JEWISH POETRY AND CULTURAL COEXISTENCE IN LATE MEDIEVAL SPAIN

JEWISH ENGAGEMENTS

Much of Jewish culture and history has been informed by the relationship Jews had with members of other religious communities. This series welcomes monographs and article collections on all aspects of Jewish culture but most especially encourages contributions which focus on Jewish religious, social, literary, scientific, and artistic relations with non-Jews from late antiquity to the early modern period. The series is intended to encompass not only Western Europe, but also Byzantium, the Caucasus, Russia, the Middle East, and Persianate world, all regions of Asia, Africa, especially Ethiopia, and the Americas. In addition, the series will consider works which address instances of invented or adopted Jewish identity, or imagined Jews.

Series Editors

Alexandra F. C. Cuffel, *Rühr Universität Bochum*
Margot Behrend Valles, *Michigan State University*
Katrin Kogman-Appel, *Westfälische Wilhelms-Universität, Münster*
Rebecca Lesses, *Ithaca College*
Micha Perry, *University of Haifa*
John V. Tolan, *Université de Nantes*

JEWISH POETRY AND CULTURAL COEXISTENCE IN LATE MEDIEVAL SPAIN

by
GREGORY B. KAPLAN

British Library Cataloguing in Publication Data
A catalogue record for this book is available from the British Library.

© 2019, Arc Humanities Press, Leeds

The authors assert their moral right to be identified as the authors of their part of this work.

Permission to use brief excerpts from this work in scholarly and educational works is hereby granted provided that the source is acknowledged. Any use of material in this work that is an exception or limitation covered by Article 5 of the European Union's Copyright Directive (2001/29/EC) or would be determined to be "fair use" under Section 107 of the U.S. Copyright Act September 2010 Page 2 or that satisfies the conditions specified in Section 108 of the U.S. Copyright Act (17 USC §108, as revised by P.L. 94-553) does not require the Publisher's permission.

ISBN (print): 9781641891479
e-ISBN (PDF): 9781641891486

www.arc-humanities.org
Printed and bound by CPI Group (UK) Ltd, Croydon, CR0 4YY

For Nuria and Andrew

CONTENTS

List of Illustrations ix

Abbreviations xv

Introduction 1

Chapter 1. The Birth of Castilian *Cuaderna Vía* Poetry 7

Chapter 2. Early Jewish *Cuaderna Vía* Poetry 27

Chapter 3. Sem Tob's *Proverbios morales*:
  The Epitome of Jewish *Cuaderna Vía* Poetry 43

Chapter 4. The Legacy of Jewish *Cuaderna Vía* Poetry 67

Conclusion 77

Index 81

LIST OF ILLUSTRATIONS

Map of Spain xi

Cloister of the Colegiata (Collegiate Church) of San Martín de Elines................xii

Thirteenth-century tomb in the cloister of the Colegiata
(Collegiate Church) of San Martín de Elines xiii

Close-up of a scallop shell carved on a thirteenth-century tomb in the
cloister of the Colegiata (Collegiate Church) of San Martín de Elines................ xiv

Close-up of a seemingly medieval wooden roof over the interior
of the Church of the Cross (in Carrión de los Condes)............................. xiv

Figure 1. Cloister of the Monastery of San Zoilo in Carrión de los Condes...........11

Figure 2. Church of San Martín in Frómista 12

Figure 3. Colegiata (Collegiate Church) of San Martín de Elines.
           View from the south (above) and from the east (right).....................14

Figure 4. Church of the Cross (in Carrión de los Condes),
           which was a synagogue in the Middle Ages..................................44

Figure 5. Interior of the Church of the Cross (in Carrión de los Condes),
           which was a synagogue in the Middle Ages..................................45

Map of Spain. (Map data © 2019 Inst. Geogr. Nacional, Google)

Cloister of the Colegiata (Collegiate Church) of San Martín de Elines.
(Photo by Gregory B. Kaplan)

Thirteenth-century tomb in the cloister of the Colegiata (Collegiate Church) of San Martín de Elines. (Photo by Gregory B. Kaplan)

Close-up of a scallop shell carved on a thirteenth-century tomb in the cloister of the Colegiata (Collegiate Church) of San Martín de Elines, which is evidence of medieval Compostelan pilgrimage in Valderredible. (Photo by Gregory B. Kaplan)

Close-up of a seemingly medieval wooden roof over the interior of the Church of the Cross (in Carrión de los Condes), which was a synagogue in the Middle Ages. (Photo by Gregory B. Kaplan)

ABBREVIATIONS

b.	born
BCE	Before Common Era
ca.	circa
CE	Common Era
d.	died
ed.	edition/editor
fl.	flourished
intro.	introduction
n.p.	no publisher
no.	number
r.	reigned
St.	saint
trans.	translated by
v.	verse/verses
vol.	volume
vols.	volumes

Unless otherwise indicated, all translations into English are my own.

INTRODUCTION

THIS BOOK OFFERS a ground-breaking perspective on Judeo-Christian coexistence in medieval Spain, in particular on the Camino de Santiago (Way of St. James), one of the most important pilgrimage routes in Europe. The concept of peaceful, parallel religious societies in medieval Spain was first described by the Spanish historian Américo Castro.[1] Castro envisioned a utopian period of cultural interchanges, but did not make an adequate case that an interconfessional Utopia surfaced in the writings of the period. In reaction to this overarching depiction of coexistence, David Nirenberg "questions the very existence of an age of peaceful and idyllic" relations by arguing that anti-Semitic violence "was a central and systemic aspect of the coexistence of majority and minorities in medieval Spain."[2] Similarly, Mark Cohen writes of "the gloomy position" of Castilian Jews during the Middle Ages.[3] While the historical records examined by Nirenberg and Mark Cohen expose the non-monolithic character of abutting belief communities, these scholars fail to take into account literary testimony of cooperation between Christians and Jews. In this book, I uncover new evidence of Judeo-Christian cooperation in Castilian monasteries on the Camino de Santiago. My book reveals that a collaborative climate endured in these monasteries as demonstrated by the transmission of *cuaderna vía* poetry from Christians to Jews.

I focus on poems written by Jews in Castilian (Spanish) during the thirteenth and fourteenth centuries that illustrate a progressive mastery of *cuaderna vía* poetry. This metrical form began to take shape within twelfth-century French monastic circles as an outgrowth of a renewed appreciation for Classical Antiquity. Much attention was paid to the Greek ruler Alexander the Great (b. 356–d. 32 BCE), whose life was recounted by clerics from the order of Cluny in narrative poems which comprised dodecasyllabic alexandrine verses. During the early thirteenth century, Castilian *cuaderna vía* poetry was created by clerics working at Castilian monasteries on the Camino de Santiago, who were influenced by French Cluniac monks invited to teach at their monastic schools. The Castilian monasteries that received Cluniac monks sought integration within Catholic Christendom by practising customs popularized by Cluny, such as the versification of liturgical hymns.[4] Castilian clerics also had an economic motivation for adapting French metrics, namely, the familiarity of alexandrine verses to French pilgrims travelling along the Camino de Santiago might encourage them to make donations.

In chapter 1, "The Birth of Castilian *Cuaderna Vía* Poetry," I explain the process by which Castilian clerics learned to adapt the rules of French versification while studying under Cluniac monks in monastic schools. At a time when Castilian was a nascent literary language, motivation for clerics to imitate French norms emerged organically as they crafted fresh compositions of alexandrine verses grouped in rhymed quatrains

---

[1] Castro, *The Structure of Spanish History*, 221–29.
[2] Nirenberg, *Communities of Violence*, 9.
[3] Cohen, *Under Crescent and Cross*, 199.
[4] On these hymns, see Evans, *Monastic Life at Cluny*, 103–7.

nicknamed *cuaderna vía*, or fourfold way. The transmission of the alexandrine verse from native speakers of Old French to native speakers of Castilian is confirmed by the treatment in early Castilian *cuaderna vía* poems of linguistic features of Old French. Castilian clerics also found appealing the *medial caesura* within the alexandrine verse, which provided a natural syntactic and respiratory pause that facilitated the recitation of lengthy narrative poems. These clerics reveal that they assimilated Old French norms to Castilian versification in their production of fourteen-syllable, rather than twelve-syllable, alexandrines. It is instructive to point out that this evolution of clerical *cuaderna vía* poetry suggests that Castilian clerics, as they came to Castilianize *cuaderna vía* techniques, also became teachers of *cuaderna vía* norms to Castilian clerics, which occurred contemporaneous to the decline of Cluny during the thirteenth century.

As scholars have established, Castilian *cuaderna vía* poems were routinely recited aloud at monasteries to pilgrims. In his critical edition of *Vida de San Millán de la Cogolla* (Life of St. Emilian Cucullatus), by Gonzalo de Berceo (b. ca. 1196–d. ca. 1260), Brian Dutton discusses this manner of public dissemination. Berceo was a cleric at the monastery of San Millán de la Cogolla, which lies today in the Spanish province of La Rioja but which was part of a thirteenth-century Castilian kingdom whose frontiers extended eastward until the Basque Country. Public readings of *Vida de San Millán* occurred not only at San Millán de la Cogolla but, as Dutton asserts, also at the many smaller churches and hospitals that were overseen by the monastery as a means of magnifying its importance to Compostelan pilgrims.[5]

Cuaderna vía poems include popular discourse as well as vignettes that highlight social mores, which indicates that the clerics who composed and recited these poems interacted with pilgrims travelling on the Camino de Santiago as well as with local populations. This interaction has been studied by scholars such as Simone Pinet, who describes *cuaderna vía* poetry as a vehicle for the "transmission of knowledge" from Christian clerics to lay people.[6] Scholars have overlooked interaction between clerics and Jews at key Castilian pilgrimage monasteries along the Camino de Santiago, a potential avenue of research that has been obscured by the sporadic appearance in *cuaderna vía* poems of anti-Semitic libels, that is, accusations that Jews were involved in heretical acts.

Well known examples of such vilification are found in *Milagros de Nuestra Señora* (Miracles of Our Lady), which was composed by Berceo around 1250 and which he or another cleric read aloud to pilgrims as M. Ana Diz posits.[7] *Milagros* is a *cuaderna vía* poem consisting of nine hundred and eleven mono-rhymed quatrains, in which Berceo narrates twenty-five episodes that communicate the importance of Marian devotion in attaining Salvation, in particular for those who commit the sins (such as fornication and theft) depicted in these episodes. Jews appear several times as figures who are religious outsiders and thus the objects of ridicule and violence. In one episode, "Cristo y

---

5 Berceo, *La "Vida de San Millán"*, 185–86. Fernando Gómez Redondo, "Origen y formulación de la lectura moderna," 82, posits that Berceo's other works were also recited aloud to pilgrims.

6 Pinet, *The Task of the Cleric*, 3.

7 Diz, *Historias de certidumbre*, 42, 47, 211–12.

los judíos de Toledo" ("Christ and the Jews of Toledo"), Jews are caught in the act of crucifying a wax figure of Christ and are subsequently massacred. This event is not historical and, like the other episodes involving Jews, is a retelling of a libel that circulated throughout Europe. In the case of Berceo's "Cristo y los judíos de Toledo," the episode centres, as Joshua Trachtenberg explains, on "[o]ne of the commonest charges against the Jews [...] [and one that originated in the] doctrine of transubstantiation [...] established at the Fourth Lateran Council in 1215."[8]

There was an economic motive for the inclusion of anti-Semitic libels that was tied to the historical evolution of pilgrimage on the Camino de Santiago, which increased dramatically during the twelfth century. In response to growing competition for donations, *cuaderna vía* poetry was refined as a tool for drawing greater numbers of pilgrims to monasteries. As a component of their education, Castilian clerics learned how to cast a wide net by composing *cuaderna vía* poems in which the vilified figures (such as the Devil, Jews, lepers, Muslims, and sorcerers) were familiar to pilgrims arriving from throughout Europe. This is confirmed by fictional episodes that depict these figures in similar terms in Castilian clerical *cuaderna vía* poems and in texts in other languages by clerics from pilgrimage centres across Europe, which indicates widespread awareness of the propagandistic value, and by extension the potential monetary benefits, of weaving invective into publicly recited works.

Of course, such value depended on latent anti-Semitism among the European populace, and this well-documented historical animus was certainly felt by lay people as well as by clerics. While clerics tapped into this anti-Semitism in order to reap economic benefits, the poems analysed in the present volume demonstrate that some Christian clerics collaborated with Jews in Castilian monasteries on the Camino de Santiago. These poems, as I demonstrate in the cases of anonymous works in chapter 2, "Early Jewish *Cuaderna Vía* Poetry," reveal that during the thirteenth century Jews began to compose *cuaderna vía* poetry, which could only have occurred through study in monastic schools with Christian clerics, who were conduits of written culture and the sole individuals capable of instructing others in this verse form. Jews living close to Castilian pilgrimage monasteries would have been aware that *cuaderna vía* poetry was recited publicly, and this motivated their interest in exploiting that medium. The fact that Jewish *cuaderna vía* poems appear in medieval and early-modern Jewish prayer books reveals why some Jews learned to compose a type of verse that was only taught in monastic schools, namely in order to produce liturgical texts that could be recited aloud.

In chapter 3, "*Proverbios morales*, the Epitome of Jewish *Cuaderna Vía* Poetry," I focus on *Proverbios morales* (Moral Proverbs), one of the most important works of medieval Castilian literature. *Proverbios morales* was written around 1350 by Sem Tob de Carrión (b. ca. 1290–d. ca. 1369). Few biographical details on Sem Tob have been uncovered, although it is known that he lived in Carrión de los Condes, a frequently visited stop on the Camino de Santiago. Sem Tob's nearly flawless Castilian *cuaderna vía* versification indicates a period of extensive study with Christian clerics. Sem Tob criticism has yet to focus on the manner by which he learned *cuaderna vía* norms, and I advance the theory

---

8 Trachtenberg, *The Devil and the Jews*, 109.

that he studied at the Cluniac monastery of San Zoilo, which was the first Castilian Cluniac monastery established on the Camino de Santiago and which owned lands on which the Jews of Carrión de los Condes lived. My theory is based on historical documents that reveal the unique position of Jews living near this monastery, who were granted the same royal privileges as Christians in 1220. Inevitably, these Jews, including Sem Tob, would have interacted with their clerical patrons.

After serving during turbulent times at the court of Alfonso XI (r. 1312–1350), Sem Tob dedicated *Proverbios morales* to Alfonso's successor on the Castilian and Leonese thrones, Pedro I (r. 1350–1369). The only poem dedicated by either a Jew or Christian to King Pedro, Sem Tob's *Proverbios morales* advocates for sensible policies and toleration toward Jews. Sem Tob also lived at a critical juncture in the history of peninsular Jewry, when the continuation of royal protection of Jewish subjects was threatened not only by the spread of anti-Semitism but also by a rise in Jewish sectarianism. This internal dispute concerning the limits of rabbinic authority intensified majority prejudices against Jews insofar as the image of a splintered Jewish faith was considered flawed compared to a supposedly unified Roman Catholicism. In calling for toleration toward Jews and an end to Jewish sectarianism, *Proverbios morales* speaks to Christian and Jewish publics. Sem Tob's composition of this poem according to *cuaderna vía* norms speaks to his involvement in an interconfessional collaborative culture that supplied him with the tools for voicing his ideas on multiple levels.

In chapter 4, "The Legacy of Jewish *Cuaderna Vía* Poetry," I examine texts from the fourteenth century onwards, including original works such as the "Coplas de Yoçef" (Couplets on Joseph) as well as fragments of thirteenth-century texts that have circulated orally outside of the Iberian Peninsula until modern times. When these poems and those analysed in previous chapters are considered together as they are for the first time in this book, they form a unique corpus of Jewish poetry whose origins are grounded in a collaboration between Christians and Jews that has not been recognized in previous scholarship. Readers will find a perspective that challenges the presumption that medieval coexistence was always "predicated upon violence," as Nirenberg asserts.[9] My analysis reveals that, in Castilian monasteries on the Camino de Santiago where *cuaderna vía* poetry was cultivated, interconfessional toleration was built on a dialogue involving Christian clerical poets writing in tandem with their Jewish counterparts. Judeo-Christian coexistence was predicated on cooperation between Jews and clerics who shared their intellectual formation over a period of time that, as demonstrated by the poems I study, was sufficient enough in length to allow for the process of education to occur repeatedly.

---

9 Nirenberg, *Communities of Violence*, 245.

Works Cited

Berceo, Gonzalo de. *Milagros de Nuestra Señora*. Edited by Michael Gerli. 5th ed. Madrid: Cátedra, 1991.
——. *Miracles of Our Lady*. Translated by Richard Terry Mount and Annette Grant Cash. Lexington: University Press of Kentucky, 1997.
——. *La "Vida de San Millán de la Cogolla": Gonzalo de Berceo. Obras completas, I.* Edited by Brian Dutton. 2nd ed. London: Tamesis, 1984.
Carrión, Sem Tob de. *Proverbios morales*. Edited by Paloma Díaz-Mas and Carlos Mota. Madrid: Cátedra, 1998.
Castro, Américo. *The Structure of Spanish History*. Translated by Edmund L. King. Princeton: Princeton University Press, 1954.
Cohen, Mark R. *Under Crescent and Cross: The Jews in the Middle Ages*. Princeton: Princeton University Press, 2008.
"Coplas de Yoçef": A Medieval Spanish Poem in Hebrew Characters. Edited and translated by Ignacio González Llubera. Cambridge: Cambridge University Press, 1935.
Diz, M. Ana. *Historias de certidumbre: los "Milagros" de Berceo*. Newark: Juan de la Cuesta, 1995.
Evans, Joan. *Monastic Life at Cluny, 910–1157*. Hamden: Archon, 1968.
Gómez Redondo, Fernando. "Origen y formulación de la lectura moderna (siglos XIII y XIV)." In *Teoría de la lectura*, edited by Pedro Aullón de Haro y María Dolores Abascal, 53–100. Málaga: Universidad de Málaga, 2006.
Nirenberg, David. *Communities of Violence: Persecution of Minorities in the Middle Ages*. Princeton: Princeton University Press, 1996.
Pinet, Simone. *The Task of the Cleric: Cartography, Translation, and Economics in Thirteenth-Century Iberia*. Toronto: University of Toronto Press, 2016.
Trachtenberg, Joshua. *The Devil and the Jews: The Medieval Conception of the Jew and its Relation to Modern Antisemitism*. New Haven: Yale University Press, 1943.

Chapter 1

THE BIRTH OF CASTILIAN *CUADERNA VÍA* POETRY

Cuaderna vía poetry was a high-culture literary by-product of the French monastic school, an academic institution that evolved over the course of the Middle Ages. The earliest French monastic schools were established in the fifth century, and their proliferation was encouraged by legislation issued by Charlemagne (b. 742–d. 814), which mandated a standardized curriculum in monastic schools. A surge in monastic foundations during the tenth century contributed to an amplification of monastic educational programs. The most important was the Benedictine monastery of Cluny in central France, which was established around 910 by William I (b. 875–d. 918), the Duque of Aquitaine. The fact that Cluny declared exclusive allegiance to the papacy helped to extend its influence internationally, well beyond that of other French monasteries.[1] With papal support, Cluniac traditions were popularized by monks who travelled to other monasteries that were, on many occasions, officially annexed to Cluny. On other occasions, the influence of Cluny was extended indirectly. One example is St. Martin of Tournai, which traces its origins to the seventh century but which was refounded in the eleventh century as one of a number of monasteries that functioned according to a "Cluniac system [...] for the proper administration of the monastery."[2] The association between Tournai and Cluny reflected a growing tendency toward adopting Cluniac norms, which encouraged the development within monasteries of intellectual pursuits. For example, among the monasteries that became Cluniac daughter houses, Saint-Bénigne, in Dijon, became a "widely influential center of monastic spirituality and education."[3] This was the historical moment when Cluniac education became normalized and centred on the practice of reading.

---

[1] According to its charter, every five years Cluny was required to "pay to Rome twelve pieces of gold for the upkeep of the candles of the Church of the Apostles. May they have as protectors the Apostles themselves, and for the defender the Pontiff of Rome" (quoted in Evans, *Monastic Life at Cluny*, 6).

[2] Hunt, *Cluny Under Saint Hugh*, 140.

[3] Melville, *The World of Medieval Monasticism*, 60.

ABSTRACT In this chapter I explain the process by which Castilian clerics learned to adapt the rules of French versification while studying under Cluniac monks in monastic schools. At a time when Castilian was a nascent literary language, motivation for clerics to imitate French norms emerged organically as they crafted fresh compositions of alexandrine verses grouped in rhymed quatrains nicknamed *cuaderna vía*, or fourfold way. The transmission of the alexandrine verse from native speakers of Old French to native speakers of Castilian is confirmed by the treatment in early Castilian *cuaderna vía* poems of linguistic features of Old French. The evolution of clerical *cuaderna vía* poetry suggests that Castilian clerics, as they came to Castilianize *cuaderna vía* techniques, also engaged in teaching *cuaderna vía* norms to new generations of clerics, which occurred contemporaneous to the decline of Cluny during the thirteenth century.

The availability of manuscripts enabled greater numbers of monks to participate in daily reading exercises that were required at Cluny according to Benedictine norms:

> The reading of books was a part of the daily life of the monastery, and brought into its tradition an element of literary culture. According to the Benedictine Rule the monks read in the cloister from the fourth to the sixth hour between Easter and October, and after Sext might either read in the cloister or rest on their beds. In the short winter days there was only time for an hour's reading; but with Lent the time was again increased. On Sundays reading was permitted at any time between the offices and meals.
>
> At Cluny, besides private reading, there was much reading aloud both in church, refectory, and chapter-house. At Septuagesima, Genesis was begun for the night office, and finished in a week; Exodus followed at Sexagesima, and it and the succeeding books of the Bible were read in both church and refectory [...]. At the Chapter part of the Benedictine Rule was read and commented on every morning, and every evening there was more reading [...].[4]

Due to the important role that silent and aloud reading played in daily life, it is no surprise that Cluny came to possess one of the great monastic libraries. Many manuscripts that formed part of the collection were produced by copyists at Cluny who, from the tenth through the twelfth centuries, may have supplied all the manuscripts "needed for the services and public reading of the abbey."[5] These manuscripts were employed as "textbooks" for clerics learning the liturgy during sessions, or "classes," which might be accompanied by oral exercises and which took place at regular intervals, that is, just as schools have functioned over the course of human history.

After spending several hours reading during the daytime, Cluniac monks continued their education at night. As Noreen Hunt explains, Cluny developed a "reputation for long nocturnal lessons," which involved frequent "occasions when marathon exercises were practiced at Cluny. During the night following the death of a brother the whole psalter was chanted during each of the first two watches except on summer nights when a hundred psalms were said."[6] The obligation for monks to read frequently was a component of monastic education that was popularized during the abbacy of Peter the Venerable (b. ca. 1092–d. 1156), who oversaw "a great revival of literature."[7] This revival gave new life to a tradition that had formed part of monastic education several centuries earlier, when a "literary enthusiasm" developed for classical texts, which were read and studied for their rhetorical value.[8] As a result of Peter's effort to widen the scope of intellectual life at his monastery during the twelfth century, the library at Cluny increased its collection dramatically, which provided monks with greater access to classical texts.[9]

---

[4] Evans, *Monastic Life at Cluny*, 98. On the Benedictine policy toward reading, see chapter 48 ("The Daily Manual Labor") of the *Holy Rule of Saint Benedict*. Ancos García (*Transmisión y recepción*, 35–36) highlights the importance afforded to the vocalization of texts during both silent and aloud reading according to the Benedictine tradition.

[5] Evans, *Monastic Life at Cluny*, 115.

[6] Hunt, *Cluny Under Saint Hugh*, 103–4.

[7] Evans, *Monastic Life at Cluny*, 108.

[8] Riché, *Education and Culture in the Barbarian West*, 498.

[9] Haskins observes that "there are many classical authors among the five hundred and seventy

Greater access to classical texts and the obligation to read contributed, in turn, to the development of a literary culture at Cluny. This phenomenon is documented by modern scholarship that confirms the link between reading and creative writing, and in this spirit new forms of poetry were cultivated at Cluny.[10] For example, the interweaving of social themes with innovative versification is evident in Latin poems such as *De contemptu mundi* (*Scorn for the World*), by the twelfth-century monk Bernard of Cluny (or Bernard of Morval). Bernard's satirical poem "is the most finished example of Cluniac prosody in its rhythmic devices, its assonances and alliterations, its repetitions and antitheses, its classical allusions and its verbal virtuosities."[11] The importance lent to the composition of verse during the abbacy of Peter, who was a skilled poet himself, impacted poetry in the French vernacular, and it should not be considered mere coincidence that one of the earliest French poems to narrate the life of Alexander the Great was written in the twelfth century by a cleric who worked within the orbit of Cluny.

The first Alexander poems in Old French were composed during the late 1100s by Lambert li Tors (fl. twelfth century) and Alexandre de Bernay (fl. twelfth century). In around 1170, Lambert's *Li Romans d'Alixandre* (Romance of Alexander) "pioneered the dodecasyllabic line in French."[12] Dodecasyllabic verses were also employed in the rendition of the Alexander story by Bernay, who hailed from the town of the same name where a Benedictine abbey had been situated since the early eleventh century. Cluny had a longstanding relationship with the abbey of Bernay, which was built under the auspices of a Cluniac monk, William of Volpiano (b. 962–d. 1031), who also served as abbot. It is likely that Alexandre de Bernay was inspired to write his Alexander poem by his exposure to Cluniac literary culture. Bernay's poem remained "enduringly popular" and inspired "numerous adaptations and *mises en prose*."[13] The use of these early Alexander poems as model texts in monastery schools would explain how other clerics learned to compose dodecasyllabic verses in French, including Guernes de Pont-Sainte-Maxence (fl. twelfth century), whose *La vie de Saint Thomas le Martyr* (Life of Saint Thomas the Martyr) recounts the life of Thomas Becket (b. 1118–d. 1170).

The first verse of Lambert's poem reveals that his work was meant to be "heard and understood," that is, through public reading.[14] Armando Petrucci argues that public reading was the manner by which texts were typically disseminated in monastic schools, and it is logical to speculate that this is how techniques related to the recitation of dodecasyllabic alexandrines were taught at Cluniac monastic schools.[15] A non-clerical visual representation of this method of instruction is found in an early fourteenth-cen-

---

volumes of the twelfth-century catalogue of Cluni, a remarkably large and complete collection for its time" (*The Renaissance of the 12th Century*, 43).

10 On the link between reading and creative writing, see Bazerman, "A Relationship between Reading and Writing" and Beji "The Importance of Reading in Creative Writing."

11 Evans, *Monastic Life at Cluny*, 112.

12 Gaunt, "Travel and Orientalism," 122.

13 Gaunt, "Travel and Orientalism," 123.

14 "entendre et oir" (Tors, 1).

15 Petrucci, *Historia de la escritura e historia de la Sociedad*, 184.

tury manuscript containing a copy of *Li Livres dou Trésor* (The Book of the Treasure), by the Italian philosopher Brunetto Latini (b. ca. 1220–d. ca. 1294). On the third folio of this manuscript, Latini is portrayed as reading *Li Livres dou Trésor* to his students.[16] This was likely the process by which French Alexander poems became widely known among Cluniac monks, whose practice of reading these poems aloud would become inexorably linked to pilgrimage in Spain.

During the twelfth century, enrolment declined in remotely located French monastery schools in favour of study in cathedral schools in urban centres including Tours, Orléans, Chartres, and Paris. At the same time, monastic education in Spain was enhanced by the arrival of French clerics, who were drawn by increased pilgrimage through northern Spain on the Camino de Santiago. This increase came in the wake of a concerted effort, led by Cluniac clerics, to publicize the existence of a shrine housing the relics of the apostle and first century martyr St. James the Greater (Santiago), which was a necessary endeavour insofar as there is no indication that Santiago was venerated in north-western Spain prior to the ninth century.

The first reference to the preaching of Santiago on the Iberian Peninsula comes from the *Breviarium apostolorum* (Breviary of the Apostles), a work from the end of the sixth or beginning of the seventh century.[17] The *Breviarium apostolorum* does not describe a pilgrimage route through northern Spain to venerate St. James, and it is plausible that the early centre of the cult of St. James was located in southern Spain. This theory is supported by the existence of a stele in the church of Santa María, in the city of Mérida, which dates from the first half of the seventh century. The stele in question contains an inscription that names the relics of St. James, which confirms for scholars such as Joaquín de Navascués and Justo Pérez de Urbel that his cult of followers was centred in Mérida prior to its establishment in Santiago. It is logical to speculate, as these scholars do, that the relics of St. James were moved north from Mérida after Islamic hegemony was established in southern Spain in the eighth century. This theory is supported by the fact that many transfers of relics occurred during the following centuries, while southern Spain was under Islamic rule, as in the cases of the relics of St. Eulogius, St. Pelagius, and St. Zoilus, which were transferred to the north from Córdoba.[18]

Writing during the last decades of the 700s, the Cantabrian monk Beato de Liébana (b. ca. 730–d. ca. 800) was the first to designate St. James as the patron saint of Spain. Although he does not mention the location of the relics of the Apostle, in a liturgical hymn dedicated to the Asturian monarch Mauregato (r. 783–788), Beato refers to James as "our protector and national patrón."[19] Several decades after Beato's hymn, and soon after the discovery around the year 800 in Galicia of the tomb of St. James (an event not

---

16 A photograph of the third folio of this manuscript is included as plate 12 by Stones ("Notes on Three Illuminated Alexander Manuscripts").

17 On the *Breviarium apostolorum*, see Pérez de Urbel, "Orígenes del culto de Santiago en España," 12–14.

18 For detailed information on these transfers, see Royo, "Las reliquias viajeras."

19 "Tutorque nobis et patronus vernulus" (Beato, *Obras completas*, 674–75). For the complete text of this hymn, see Beato, *Obras completas*, 672–75.

Figure 1. Cloister of the Monastery of San Zoilo in Carrión de los Condes.
(Photo by Gregory B. Kaplan)

narrated until 1077), pilgrimage to north-western Spain is first documented in a French martyrology from the early ninth century.[20]

The Camino de Santiago became internationally famous upon the completion of the *Liber Sancti Jacobi* (Book of St. James), or *Codex Calixtinus* (Codex of Callixtus), a mid-twelfth-century illuminated guidebook for pilgrims to which several clerics contributed, including the French Cluniac monk, Aymeric Picard (fl. twelfth century), who wrote a large portion of the work. The guidebook was commissioned by a Galician Cluniac cleric, Diego Gelmírez (b. ca. 1069–d. ca. 1140), who served as bishop and archbishop of the Archdiocese of Santiago de Compostela during much of the first half of the twelfth century. In listing churches and monasteries at which pilgrims could find repose in France and Spain, including official Cluniac daughter monasteries and those that came within the orbit of Cluny, *Codex Calixtinus* imprinted the Cluniac brand on the Camino de San-

---

[20] The first narration of the discovery of the tomb of St. James in Galicia is found in the *Concordia de Antealtares* (*Accord of Antealtares*), a copy of which made in 1435 is housed in Spain at the Universidad de Santiago de Compostela (on the *Concordia*, see López Alsina, "Concordia de Antealtares"). On the French martyrology in question, see Pérez de Urbel, "Orígenes del culto de Santiago en España," 25–26.

Figure 2. Church of San Martín in Frómista. (Photo by Gregory B. Kaplan)

tiago and laid the foundation for the transfer of Cluniac culture to Spain, in particular to Castile, at a historical moment during which French monastic life was in decline.

This transfer commenced during the reign of Alfonso VI (b. ca. 1040–d. 1109), who became king of León in 1065. After the death of his brother in 1072, Alfonso ascended the thrones of Castile and Galicia as well. During his rule over Castile, León and Galicia, Alfonso VI ceded control of monasteries to the Order of Cluny, with which he possessed a link by virtue of his marriage to the niece of Hugh the Great (b. 1024–d. 1109), who served as abbot of Cluny from 1049 until his death. Alfonso's desire to ensure adherence to Cluniac norms in the monasteries situated within his realm is revealed by his "gratitude to Hugh [...] for sending him monks."[21] Furthermore, in the same letter to Hugh in which he expresses this gratitude, Alfonso VI also pledges to "double his alms to Cluny in the future."[22]

The first monastery to be donated by Alfonso VI to Cluny was San Zoilo, in the town of Carrión de los Condes, which became a daughter monastery in 1076.[23] Other northern

---

21 Delaruelle, "The Crusading Idea in Cluniac Literature," 196.
22 Delaruelle, "The Crusading Idea in Cluniac Literature," 196.
23 Pérez Celada, *Documentación del monasterio de San Zoilo de Carrión*, 16. The document that

Castilian monasteries became daughter monasteries of Cluny in the years that followed, and Cluny would establish a significant presence on the Camino de Santiago, including:

> through the influence of Cluny on the observance of many monasteries which were never actually incorporated in the order. An example may be found in the history of Sahagún, a centre of Cluniac observance which impregnated the monasteries of León and Castile with the same spirit without ever being incorporated in the order.[24]

An additional example is the Church of San Martín in the town of Frómista, which was originally built as part of a monastery that was annexed to San Zoilo in 1112, "thus putting Frómista much more into the sphere of Cluniac influence than it had been."[25]

The history of San Martín de Elines, a former Castilian monastery in what is today the municipality of Valderredible in southern Cantabria, was also shaped by Cluny.[26] San Martín de Elines is located on a pilgrimage route that came into existence during the sixth century, well before pilgrimage to Santiago is documented. For three centuries, this route was travelled by followers of the cult of Emilian (b. 475– d. 575), who was later canonized as St. Emilian Cucullatus (and whose feast day is November 12). Emilian (in Spanish, "Millán") was a hermit who lived with other ascetics in rock-cut churches in Valderredible, and his relics were venerated there from the time of his death until they were moved to their current location, San Millán de la Cogolla, around the time this Benedictine monastery was founded in the early 900s. By this point in history, the route to visit the relics of San Millán in Valderredible had transformed into a feeder route, or the Ruta Románica (Romanesque Route), for pilgrims travelling from the Cantabrian coast to Burgos in order to join the principal Compostelan route, the Camino Francés (French Way).[27] The Ruta Románica receives its name from the many Romanesque churches in its vicinity, with the most important being the Benedictine monastery of San Martín de Elines, some hundred and thirty kilometres to the north-west of San Millán de la Cogolla. Like San Millán de la Cogolla, San Martín de Elines was founded in the tenth century and during the twelfth century the structure that stands today was built in the Romanesque style that was popularized by Cluny. Although neither San Millán de la Cogolla nor San Martín de Elines officially became Cluniac daughter monasteries, both were influenced by Cluniac traditions. Cluniac monks are known to have visited San Millán de la Cogolla and, in the case of San Martín de Elines, the monastery was situated within the orbit of Cluniac influence insofar as Cluny controlled lands in the nearby towns of Aguilar de Campóo and Cervatos (where a Romanesque monastery was also built in the twelfth century).[28]

---

records the monastery's foundation recognizes the situation of San Zoilo on the Camino de Santiago (Pérez Celada, *Documentación del monasterio de San Zoilo de Carrión*, 4).

24 Hunt, *Cluny Under Saint Hugh*, 127.

25 Shaver-Crandell and Gerson, *The Pilgrim's Guide to Santiago de Compostela*, 196.

26 In 1541, San Martín de Elines lost its monastic status and was named a *colegiata* (collegiate church).

27 See Kaplan, *El culto a San Millán*, for in-depth discussions of the cult of St. Millán in Valderredible and the origins of the Ruta Románica.

28 On the Cluniac influence at the monastery of San Millán de la Cogolla, see Donovan, *The Liturgical Drama in Medieval Spain*, 52.

14 CHAPTER 1

Figure 3.
Colegiata (Collegiate Church)
of San Martín de Elines.
View from the south (above)
and from the east (right).
(Photos by Gregory B. Kaplan)

The study of French versification within Castilian monastic schools on the Camino de Santiago contributed to the production of clerical *cuaderna vía* poems written in Castilian, including a dozen texts during the thirteenth century. Clerical *cuaderna vía* poems in Castilian centre primarily on religious figures, including the Virgin and a variety of saints, although exceptions include Apollonius of Tyre, a legendary classical character, Fernán González (d. 970), the first count of Castile, and Alexander the Great. Some of these poems are anonymous, although the most prolific *cuaderna vía* poet, Berceo, who authored nine works, is historically documented as having worked at San Millán de la Cogolla, which was a key Compostelan pilgrimage monastery on the eastern fringe of Castile.[29]

While scholars have posited that Christian clerical poets who wrote *cuaderna vía* poems in Castilian learned *cuaderna vía* versification at the University of Palencia, including Berceo and the anonymous author of *Libro de Alexandre* (*Book of Alexander*), no direct evidence exists of such training.[30] With respect to *Libro de Alexandre*, a Castilian retelling of the Alexander legend composed during the early thirteenth century, Peter Such and Richard Rabone rightly underscore that Palencia, "is not mentioned [...] whilst other centres of learning are named as such in stanzas 2582–2583."[31] In fact, *Libro de Alexandre* may be directly linked to monastic schools on the Camino de Santiago. Elimio Alarcos Llorach asserts that *Libro de Alexandre* contains clues as to the provenance of the author, who may have hailed from the region in northern Spain between Burgos and Soria as revealed by references to that region in the poem.[32] If true, this would situate the composition of *Libro de Alexandre* on a feeder route to the Camino Francés known as the Camino Castellano-Aragonés (Castilian-Aragonese Way). A clue that points to the author's clerical education is contained in verse 2 of *Libro de Alexandre*, which proclaims that the work is "born of the clergy's learning."[33] The Spanish word used in the poem for "clergy's learning," or "clerezía," is a clear reference to the so-called *mester de clerecía* (which can be translated as "cleric's craft"), a term that refers to the study and composition of *cuaderna vía* poetry. There is every reason to speculate, therefore, that the author of *Libro de Alexandre* was a cleric.

Such and Rabone posit that "the poet's knowledge of and access to a wealth of Alexander material points to an association with an institution possessing an extensive library, such as one of the great Castilian monasteries."[34] It would have been in such an extensive monastic collection, rather than the library collection of the recently opened

---

29 In contemporary documents from San Millán de la Cogolla, Berceo is called a "capellan" (chaplain) and a "clerigo" (cleric) (Peña de San José, "Documentos del convento de San Millán de la Cogolla," 85, 90, 91).

30 Scholars who make this claim include Rico, "La clerecía del mester," 10; Dutton, "French Influences," 79–93; and Uría Maqua, *Panorama crítico*, 57–69.

31 *Book of Alexander*, trans. Such and Rabone, 6. The "centres of learning" mentioned in quatrains 2582–83 include Paris, Pavia, Milan, Burgundy, Vienna, and Bologna. On the linguistic features of *Libro de Alexandre* that enlist it as a Castilian text, see Alarcos Llorach, *Investigaciones*, 54.

32 Alarcos Llorach, *Investigaciones*, 54–57.

33 *Book of Alexander*, 85 (v. 2b); "ca es de clerezía" (*Libro de Alexandre*, 130 [v. 2b]).

34 *Book of Alexander*, trans. Such and Rabone, 11.

University of Palencia (around 1210), where the author acquired a familiarity with Bernay's rendition of the Alexander tale, which was "a major source of descriptive material" for *Libro de Alexandre*.[35] This monastic library would have also possessed a copy of Lambert's *Li Romans d'Alixandre* (and other French works comprising dodecasyllabic verses such as Pont-Sainte-Maxence's *La vie de Saint Thomas*), as well as *Alexandreis*, a twelfth century French version of the Alexander tale by Gautier de Châtillon, with these texts also providing source material for the cleric who composed *Libro de Alexandre*.[36]

The type of instruction that occurred at Palencia according to scholars who claim that *cuaderna vía* poets were educated there also occurred in monastic schools. For example, Isabel Uría Maqua asserts that the influence on *Libro de Alexandre* of *Verbiginale* (On Verbs), a Latin treatise on Castilian morphology that formed part of the curriculum at Palencia, indicates that *Libro de Alexandre* was composed at that university.[37] Uría Maqua argues that this influence surfaces in the initial quatrain of *Libro de Alexandre*, when the poet "proclaims that it is necessary for the wise man to transmit his knowledge to the ignorant ones"[38]:

> My lords, should you wish to engage my services,
> I would most readily serve you with my craft;
> a man must be generous with what he knows
> —if not, he might fall into blame and criticism.[39]

While these lines may recall a theme discussed in the introduction to *Verbiginale* as Uría Maqua claims, a more convincing argument may be made that the first six quatrains of *Libro de Alexandre* incorporate a medieval technique known as *accessus ad auctores*.

The *accessus ad auctores*, as Amaia Arizaleta observes, "was widely disseminated during the late twelfth century."[40] Although the employment of the *accessus ad auctores* technique varied, its essential components are identified by Edwin Quain:

> The custom of medieval commentators on classical authors of prefixing to their works a *schema* [is] generally called an *accessus* [...]. In such a prefatory note they treated of items such as the following: *vita auctoris, titulus operis, intentio scribentis, materia operis, utilitas*, and *cui parti philosophiae supponatur*. In different works the number of these items might be curtailed or expanded, but the common purpose of providing an introductory summary to the work in question, is present in all forms of the *accessus*.[41]

As textual evidence reveals, this technique was taught in Castilian monastic schools to clerics such as the author of *Libro de Alexandre*.

---

35 Michael, *The Treatment of Classical Material*, 23.
36 On these sources, see *Book of Alexander*, trans. Such and Rabone, 30–32.
37 Uría Maqua, *Panorama crítico*, 57–69.
38 "declara la necesidad de que el sabio transmita sus saberes a los ignorantes" (Uría Maqua, *Panorama crítico*, 59).
39 *Book of Alexander*, 85 (v. 1a–d). "Señores, si queredes mi serviçio prender, / querríavos de grado servir de mi mester; / deve de lo que sabe omne largo seer, / si non, podríe en culpa e en riebto caer" (*Libro de Alexandre*, 129 [v. 1a–d]).
40 "conoció una gran difusión a finales del siglo XII" (Arizaleta, "El Exordio del *Libro de Alexandre*," 56).
41 Quain, "The Medieval Accessus Ad Auctores," 215.

The opening quatrains of *Libro de Alexandre* confirm that the poet was capable of incorporating the components of the *accessus ad auctores*:

> The craft I bring is refined, it is no minstrel's work,
> a craft without fault, born of the clergy's learning:
> to compose rhyming verse in the four-line form,
> with counted syllables—an act of great mastery.
> Whoever wants to listen, I believe with all my heart,
> will gain from me delight and finally great contentment.
> He will learn of fine deeds of which he may tell
> and through it he will come to be known by many.
> I wish not to offer you a great prologue or introduction,
> but to bring you without delay to my subject.
> May the Creator give us the benefit of great learning;
> if in some way we err, may He grant us His aid.
> I want to read a book about a worthy pagan king,
> about a great-hearted man of highest valour.
> He conquered the whole world and held it in his grip.
> If I succeed, I shall hold myself no mean writer.
> Prince Alexander, who was the king of Greece,
> who was noble and courageous and of great wisdom,
> defeated Porus and Darius, two kings of great power;
> never did he have a friendship with any ignoble man.[42]

While the poet does not mention his name, in the spirit of the *vita auctoris* he does assert that he is learned in *cuaderna vía* techniques ("The craft I bring is refined [...] with counted syllables—an act of great mastery"), and in keeping with the *accessus ad auctores* he also reveals: the title of his work, or *titulus operis* ("I want to read a book about [...] Prince Alexander"); his intent, or *intentio scribentis* ("Whoever wants to listen, I believe with all my heart, / will gain from me delight and finally great contentment"); his subject, or *materia operis* ("a book about a worthy pagan king [...] [who] conquered the whole world and held it in his grip"); the benefit to the reader, or *utilitas* ("He will learn of fine deeds of which he may tell / and through it he will come to be known by many"); and the philosophical foundation of the work, or *cui parti philosophiae supponatur* ("May the Creator give us the benefit of great learning / if in some way we err, may He grant us His aid").[43]

---

[42] *Book of Alexander*, 85 (v. 2a-6d). "Mester traigo fermoso, non es de joglaría, / mester es sin pecado, ca es de clerezía / fablar curso rimado por la quaderna vía, / a sílabas contadas, ca es grant maestría. / Qui oir lo quisiere, a todo mi creer, / avrá de mí solaz, en cabo grant plazer, / aprendrá buenas gestas que sepa retraer, / averlo an por ello muchos a connoçer. / Non vos quiero grant prólogo nin grandes nuevas fer, / luego a la materia me vos quier' acoger; / el Crïador nos dexe bien apresos seer, / si en algo pecarmos, Él nos deñe valer. / Quiero leer un livro d'un rey noble, pagano, / que fue de grant esfuerço, de coraçón loçano, / conquiso tod'el mundo, metiólo so su mano; / terném, si lo cumpliere, por non mal escrivano. / Del prínçep' Alexandre que fue rëy de Greçia, / que fue franc' e ardit, e de grant sabïençia; / vençió Poro e Dario, dos reys de grant potençia, / nunca con avol omne ovo su atenençia" (*Libro de Alexandre*, 130–34 [v. 2a-6d]).

[43] An alternative identification of the components of the *accessus ad auctores* in the opening quatrains to *Libro de Alexandre* is offered by Arizaleta, "El Exordio del *Libro de Alexandre*," 58.

The poet's ability to present *Libro de Alexandre* in terms of the *accessus ad auctores* speaks to a Cluniac influence on his academic training. The fact that the popularization of the *accessus ad auctores* technique can be attributed to *Dialogus super auctores* (Dialogue on Authors), a work produced by a Cluniac cleric, Conrad de Hirsau (b. ca. 1070–d. ca. 1150), makes it likely that the technique was taught at Cluniac daughter monasteries. It is logical to speculate that this is where clerics such as the author of *Libro de Alexandre* would have learned the *accessus ad auctores* as part of a curriculum that is depicted in other Castilian *cuaderna vía* poems linked to the Camino de Santiago.

In the second quatrain of *Milagros*, Berceo identifies himself as a "maestro," which can be translated as "teacher," and as such an indication, as Pablo Ancos posits, that *Milagros* and Berceo's other works were used by the author as textbooks for instructing clerics at San Millán de la Cogolla.[44] Further evidence that *cuaderna vía* poems were taught surfaces in *Libro de miseria del omne* (Book of the Man's Wretchedness), a late thirteenth-century anonymous work whose only textual witness was found by a labourer in the early twentieth century hidden inside of San Martín de Elines.[45] *Libro de miseria del omne* consists of 502 quatrains with consonant rhyme. Like other Christian clerical *cuaderna vía* works, *Libro de miseria del omne* was composed in order to be read aloud, as announced in the opening quatrain: "All who comprehend come and be with me, / and you will always comprehend as long as you listen to what I say."[46] The use of rhyme to distinguish quatrains facilitated the memorization of clerical *cuaderna vía* works such as *Libro de miseria del omne*, and further enhanced the appeal of these works to pilgrims who could also utilize rhyme to help memorize the verses they heard.

The moralizing theme of *Libro de miseria del omne*, which centres on ways to combat the tribulations of human existence, is communicated on occasions in terms that evoke the importance of academic training. For example, in a section titled "On the types of study in which man engages" ("De variis hominum studiis"), the poet underscores the place of study in learning to overcome poverty: "You have heard much in favour of the one who desires great wisdom, / what he has studied can be of great worth; / I must tell you, if you please, of the one who wishes to be wealthy: / no one can get rich just by sitting around!"[47] On another occasion, the poet praises the work of good teachers in contributing to improved health: "Moreover, good teachers select

---

44 Berceo, *Milagros*, 69 (v. 2a); Mount and Cash translate the term "maestro" as "Master" (Berceo, *Miracles*, 21 [v. 2a]).

45 Although there is divergence regarding the date of composition of *Libro de miseria de omne*, with Connolly arguing in favour of the early thirteenth century (*Translation and Poetization in the Quaderna Vía*, 108) and Alvar arguing in favour of the late fourteenth century (*Poesía española medieval*, 332), there is a general consensus, as Cuesta Serrano explains (*Libro de miseria de omne*, 38), that *Libro de miseria de omne* was written at the very end of the thirteenth century or the very beginning of the fourteenth century.

46 "Todos los que vos preciades venit a seer comigo, / más vos preciaredes siempre si oyerdes lo que digo" (*Libro de miseria del omne*, 83 [v. 1a–b]).

47 "Oístes muchas razones del que quier mucho saber, / lo que ha studïado quánto le puede valer; / dezir vos he, si vos plaze, del que quiere enrequeçer: / ¡ninguno non será rico omne por siempre al sol yacer!" (*Libro de miseria del omne*, 104 [v. 87a–d]).

the herbs to pick, / and they mix them with spices and grind them, / in order to make jam and syrup to drink / and give to the sick so that they can be healthy."[48] At a different juncture in the work, the poet appears to recall the Cluniac obligation to read at all hours by declaring that "Whoever desires great wisdom" must "keep vigil by studying many things day and night."[49]

As evidenced by his use of Latin and his expertise in a variety of fields, the author of *Libro de miseria de omne* was an educated cleric. Allusions to the monastic school at San Martín de Elines where this cleric studied are found in medieval texts discovered in the early twentieth century in the same collection of manuscripts that includes *Libro de miseria de omne*. The sole textual witness to *Libro de miseria de omne* is a copy made during the fourteenth or fifteenth centuries that occupies folios 7r–53r and folios 55r–79r of a manuscript housed as M-77 by the Biblioteca Menéndez Pelayo in Santander. The 150 folios in this manuscript contain a variety of medieval texts that centre on religious themes. One of these texts, which occupies folios 104r–115v of M-77, includes references to a monastic program of study. The topic is introduced in the opening paragraphs of this text, when the anonymous author writes: "A great deal of diligent study should be performed by every cleric so that he knows and comprehends what is required according to his order and so he lives by the rule to which he is bound and mandated by his order."[50] Further on in this text, the author depicts what may have been norms for instructing clerics in public speaking:

> He [the cleric] must be very attentive to what he says so that it comes out of his heart. If one talks to a gentleman, he should do it honestly and sanely so that they do not think of him as simple; and he should be even more careful when he is before God and his angels. The same care should be given if, by chance, he is in the plaza speaking with people, and he should be much more careful with God, to whom nothing is hidden.[51]

It is interesting to speculate that the reference to clerics in the "plaza speaking with people" included occasions on which *cuaderna vía* poetry was publicly recited to pilgrims who stopped at San Martín de Elines while travelling the Ruta Románica.

---

48 "Demás los buenos maestros fazen las yerbas cojer, / mésclanlas con especïas e fázenlas bien moler, / donde avrán letuarios e xarope pora veber / e dar a los enfermos, que puedan salud aver" (*Libro de miseria del omne*, 141 [v. 239a–d]).

49 "Quien quïer mucho saber [...] escodriñar muchas cosas, noch e día a velar" (*Libro de miseria del omne*, 103 [v. 80a–b]).

50 "Mucho grand estudio e deligencia debe toda persona eclesiastica saber e conoscer a lo que es obligado segunsu Orden porque biba ordenada mente en orden segun es obligado e le manda su orden" (*Manuscritos de Valderredible*, ed. Berzosa Guerrero, 250).

51 "Debe estar muy atento a lo que dize por la boca que lo venga asi pensando lo en el corazon. Quien aqui piense que si por ventura esta diese ante algun sennor por mas muy gran diligencia por estar honesta mente e fablar cuerda mente por que non le oviesen por sinple pues quanto mayor estudio debe poner quando esta ante dios e sus angeles e si por aventurado quando fuese emendado en la plaza de algun destierro abria gran verguenza de los onbres pues quantomas la debe aver de dios al que non se lo asconde nada" (*Manuscritos de Valderredible*, ed. Berzosa Guerrero, 254).

Another text found with *Libro de miseria de omne*, which occupies folios 143r–143v of manuscript M-77, narrates the foundation of the Carthusian Order, which occurred at the conclusion of a class that had taken place in a Parisian monastic school:

> It is said that in the Paris school there was a person of very good reputation and, when he died, the students paid him a great tribute. A deacon gave the fourth lesson, which began: "Miguel, please respond." The one who died said: "There was a trial that scared everyone." A good person who was there told the one who was giving the lesson: "Start the lesson again." The deacon said: "Miguel, please respond." The one who died said: "I am in court now." The other one repeated: "Start the lesson for a third time." The deacon said: "Miguel, please respond." And the one who died said: "I am damned." All those who were there were very frightened of this, and said: "If such a good person was condemned, what will become of us?" And so began the holy Order of the Carthusians, who do not eat meat and who abstain from many things, do penance, and live very saintly lives.[52]

Although this episode does not involve the Order of Cluny, its depiction may have served at San Martín de Elines as a model for conducting classes in which teachers solicited responses from students.

The knowledge of this Parisian episode speaks to the broader influence of French monastic culture on academic training at Castilian monasteries. Direct testimony that training was imparted at these monasteries by native speakers of Old French is revealed in the frequency of apocope, or loss of word-final vowels, in Castilian *cuaderna vía* poems. Apocope traces its origins to the medieval evolution of spoken Latin into Old French, in particular as a consequence of the popularization of one of a number of Germanic "speech-habits that are believed to have affected the pronunciation of the Latin of 'Francia.'"[53] One of these speech-habits was "the strong expiratory stress of Germanic," which was adopted by many speakers in regions of Franco-German contact.[54] Due to the popularization of this tendency, Franks speaking Latin in the early Middle Ages "applied the stresses in the right places, but made them so heavy that some syllables preceding the stress were 'swallowed' (syncopation), while the syllables which followed it were reduced drastically."[55] As a result of this reduction, the loss of final vowels occurred.

This phenomenon has been examined by P. B. Marcou, who finds that the adoption in spoken medieval French of the "strong expiratory stress of Germanic" produced a

---

[52] "Dize que en el estudio de paris avia una persona de muy buena fama e como a la muerte los estudiantes le fiziesen muy gran onra diciendo un diacono la cuarta lecion que comienza rresponde michi dixo aquel finado e juicio ovo e todos espantados del fecho dizo una buena persona que alli estaba al que dezia la lecion comienza otra vez esa lecion e dixo el finado en juicio esto e dixo comienza tercera vez edixo el finado condenado so E todos quantos alli estaban muy espantados de tal fecho dezian pues si persona de tanto bien como esta fue condenada que sera de nos otros e de alli comenzo la santa orden de los cartuxos los quales non comen carne e facen otras muchas astinendias e asperazas e biben muy santa mente" (*Manuscritos de Valderredible*, ed. Berzosa Guerrero, 300).

[53] Rickard, *A History of the French Language*, 12.

[54] Rickard, *A History of the French Language*, 13.

[55] Rickard, *A History of the French Language*, 13.

debilitating effect on unstressed syllables, namely, the loss of syllables preceding and following stressed syllables.[56] Grounding himself in *La Chanson de Roland* (The Song of Roland), the works of Chrétien de Troyes and François Villon, and Jean de Meun's *Le Roman de la Rose* (The Romance of the Rose), Marcou examines the impact on apocope of the debilitating effect in question and confirms that an acoustic phenomenon that continues to characterize French until today became a permanent feature of that language during the thirteenth and fourteenth centuries. This reduction culminated in the "absolute rule that in the development of the Latin of northern France to early O[ld] F[rench], final unstressed syllables *all* disappeared."[57] The loss of final unstressed syllables included the loss of word-final vowels, except in cases of final unstressed syllables containing the vowel /a/, and when the final unstressed vowel "was needed to support a group of consonants which could not otherwise be articulated [or] was in hiatus with the preceding stressed vowel."[58]

As Marcou and Peter Rickard have demonstrated, written testimony of the loss of final unstressed vowels first surfaces in eleventh century texts such as *La Chanson de Roland* and *La Vie de Saint Alexis* (The Life of Saint Alexis).[59] Rafael Lapesa asserts that this was precisely the time when, "the syllabic structure of Spanish was [...] particularly vulnerable to the effect of apocope."[60] Prior to the middle of the eleventh century, "the Romance spoken in the north of the Peninsula was—with the exception of Ribagorza and Catalunya—extremely conservative with respect to final vowels."[61] The arrival to northern Spain during the eleventh century of Cluniac monks, Lapesa argues, created the conditions necessary for apocope to become a widespread phenomenon, including along the Camino de Santiago. The Old French norms of pronunciation employed by Cluniac monks, which were undoubtedly perceived as high-culture norms by Castilian clerics, thus caused a weakening of final vowels in spoken and written Castilian. Indeed, this was the historical moment when King Alfonso VI worked with Hugh the Great to attract larger numbers of Cluniac monks. The prestige lent to the speech of "monks and clerics renowned as saints and learned men," and by extension the prestige lent to their system of written syllabification that incorporated the loss of final vowels, encouraged the adoption of apocope by clerics studying in Castilian monastic schools.[62]

---

56 Marcou, "The Origins of the Rule Forbidding Hiatus," 333.

57 Rickard, *A History of the French Language*, 14.

58 Rickard, *A History of the French Language*, 14.

59 For example, Rickard points out several instances of the incorporation of the loss of final vowels into the versification of *La Vie de Saint Alexis*, in which "we find the words *imagine, ángele, vírgine* occurring in consecutive lines (v. 87–89) in metrical circumstances which make it clear that there was only *one* syllable after the stress" (*A History of the French Language*, 33).

60 "la estructura silábica del español ofrecía [...] condiciones propicias a la apócope" (Lapesa, "La apócope," 197).

61 "El romance que se hablaba en el Norte de la Península se mostró—salvo en Ribagorza y Cataluña—sumamente conservador respecto a las vocales finales" (Lapesa, "La apócope," 188).

62 "monjes y clérigos con fama de santos y doctos" (Lapesa, "La apócope," 198).

Although apocope is evident in Castilian texts from the early eleventh century, Lapesa asserts that an "intensification of the phenomenon" during the twelfth century may be attributed to instruction by Cluniac clerics in monastic schools on the Camino de Santiago.[63] These monastic schools were conduits by which apocope of final /-e/ gained a foothold in Castilian, before ultimately disappearing in the fourteenth century after the influence of Cluny had waned. While it remained in vogue, apocope was incorporated into the versification of thirteenth-century Christian clerical *cuaderna vía* poems such as Berceo's *Milagros*, in which this phenomenon is evident in the loss of -e in terms like "verament" (rather than *veramente*) and "cort" (rather than *corte*).[64] As Castile fortified its political hegemony, prestige was ultimately afforded to Castilian norms. By the middle of the fourteenth century, apocope became associated with rustic speech as demonstrated by the discourse of the country women (*serranas*) in *Libro de buen amor* (*The Book of Good Love*) by Juan Ruiz (fl. early 14th century), a *cuaderna vía* work composed around 1330.[65]

Norms for *cuaderna vía* versification are described in the second quatrain of *Libro de Alexandre* and the fourth quatrain of *Libro de miseria de omne*. The two descriptions centre on rhyme and syllabic computation:

> The craft I bring is refined, it is no minstrel's work,
> a craft without fault, born of the clergy's learning:
> to compose rhyming verse in the four-line form,
> with counted syllables—an act of great mastery.[66]

> Anyone who wishes to understand this book
> should be aware that the key is to know well how to divide syllables,
> because it is by counting syllables, which is the art of rhyming,
> that the fourfold way is achieved.[67]

On both occasions the poets identify a skill, counting syllables in Castilian, which required a mastery of grammar, a subject that the author of *Libro de Alexandre* declares he has learned thoroughly: "I understand grammar well."[68] In addition to Castilian grammar, clerical *cuaderna vía* poets required extensive training in the manipulation of synalepha and hiatus (or dialepha). Synalepha describes a phenomenon in spoken Castilian that is reproduced when counting syllables by merging word-final syllables ending in vowels with succeeding syllables beginning with vowels (as in the phrase, "¿có-mo_es-

---

63 "intensificación del fenómeno" (Lapesa, "La apócope," 195).
64 Respectively, Berceo, *Milagros*, 69, v. 1d (truly) and 74, v. 30c (court).
65 On the decline of apocope in Castilian, see Lapesa, "La apócope," 221–24.
66 *Book of Alexander*, 85 (v. 2a–d); "Mester traigo fermoso, non es de joglaría, / mester es sin pecado, ca es de clerezía / fablar curso rimado por la quaderna vía, / a sílabas contadas, ca es grant maestría" (*Libro de Alexandre*, 130–31 [v. 2a–d]).
67 "Onde todo omne que quisiere este libro bien pasar / mester es que las palabras sepa bien silabificar, / ca por sílavas contadas, que es arte de rimar, / e por la quaderna vía su curso quïer finar" (*Libro de miseria de omne*, 84 [v. 4a–4d]).
68 *Book of Alexander*, 93 (v. 40a); "Entiendo bien gramática" (*Libro de Alexandre*, 145 [v. 40a]).

tás?" [how are you?], in which "mo_es" typically counts as one syllable). Synalepha is a natural feature of Castilian speech, and is employed when determining syllabic count in Renaissance italianate poetry, although synalepha is not a characteristic feature of thirteenth-century *cuaderna vía* poetry, in which it is prevented by the employment of hiatus.

The fact that synalepha was typically suppressed by authors of thirteenth-century Castilian *cuaderna vía* poems is evident in the regularity of verses that can only contain fourteen syllables if synalepha is discounted, that is, if the separation of adjacent vowels into two syllables, or hiatus, is the norm.[69] The extreme case is Berceo, who completely suppresses synalepha in works such as *Milagros* (for example, "que suya era quita" [v. 86d]; "quando ixió de casa" [v. 92c]; "mas apello a Christo" [v. 93b]), including in cases of identical vowels (for example, "fue en una mongía" [v. 76a]; "que siempre fue e éslo" [v. 78b]; "valient una agalla" [v. 87c]).[70] During the fourteenth century, the use of hiatus fell out of fashion and synalepha was employed in *cuaderna vía* works such as Ruiz's *Libro de buen amor*.

By providing pilgrims with entertainment and instruction during a break from travelling, Castilian clerical *cuaderna vía* poetry contributed to a surge in Compostelan pilgrimage during the thirteenth century, which in turn transformed the towns near pilgrimage monasteries into busting commercial centres. The growth of towns along the Camino de Santiago attracted new residents, including Jews arriving from Islamic controlled southern Spain. These Jews joined extant Jewish communities or formed new ones, and historical documentation confirms the presence of Jewish communities in Castilian centres of Compostelan pilgrimage, including Burgos, Carrión de los Condes, Castrojeriz and Frómista.[71] In such places, as Robert Chazan asserts, "real isolation was simply not possible [...]. These smaller urban enclaves fostered enhanced contact between Jews and their Christian contemporaries. Moreover, the Jewish neighbourhoods—like the parallel clusters of other groups—were by no means exclusively Jewish."[72] Indeed, with the exception of Burgos these were and continue to be small towns and, as will be explained in the following chapter, there are solid grounds for concluding that contact between Christians and Jews occurred on a regular basis and that such contact involved the transmission of *cuaderna vía* poetry.

---

69 On the absence of synalepha in thirteenth-century clerical *cuaderna vía* poetry, see Arnold, "Synalepha in Old Spanish Poetry."

70 "that it did not belong to the angels" (*Miracles*, 33 [v. 86d]); "When the sexton left the monastery" (*Miracles*, 34 [v. 92c]); "but I appeal to Christ" (*Miracles*, 34 [v. 93b]); "was in a monastery" (*Miracles*, 32 [v. 76a]); "who always was and is" (*Miracles*, 32 [v. 78b]); "even a little" (*Miracles* [v. 87c]); the translations into English are by Mount and Cash). The corresponding page numbers to these verses in *Milagros*, ed. Gerli, are as follows: 85, 87, 87, 83, 84, and 85.

71 On this documentation, see Soifer Irish, *Jews and Christians in Medieval Castile*, 56–63.

72 Chazan, *Reassessing Jewish Life in Medieval Europe*, 183–84.

Works Cited

Alarcos Llorach, Emilio. *Investigaciones sobre el Libro de Alexandre*. Madrid: Consejo Superior de Investigaciones Científicas, 1948.
Alvar, Manuel, ed. *Poesía española medieval*. 2nd ed. Madrid: Cupsa, 1978.
Ancos García, Pablo. *Transmisión y recepción primarias de la poesía del mester de clerecía*. Valencia: Universitat de València, 2012.
Arizaleta, Amaia. "El Exordio del *Libro de Alexandre*." *Revista de Literatura Medieval* 9 (1997): 47–60.
Arnold, H. H. "Synalepha in Old Spanish Poetry: Berceo." *Hispanic Review* 4 (1936): 141–58.
Bazerman, Charles. "A Relationship between Reading and Writing: The Conversational Model." *College English* 41, no. 6 (February 1980): 656–61.
Beato de Liébana. *Obras completas de Beato de Liébana*. Edited by Joaquín González Echegaray, Alberto del Campo, and Leslie G. Freeman. Madrid: Biblioteca de Autores Católicos, 1995.
Beji, Yagouta. "The Importance of Reading in Creative Writing." *International Journal of Humanities and Cultural Studies* 3, no. 1 (2016). Accessed November 20, 2018. https://www.ijhcs.com/index.php/ijhcs.
Berceo, Gonzalo de. *Milagros de Nuestra Señora*. Edited by Michael Gerli. 5th ed. Madrid: Cátedra, 1991.
———. *Miracles of Our Lady*. Translated by Richard Terry Mount and Annette Grant Cash. Lexington: University Press of Kentucky, 1997.
Bernay, Alexandre de. *Le Roman d'Alexandre*. Edited by Edward Cooke Armstrong. Paris: Poche, 1994.
Book of Alexander (Libro de Alexandre). Translated by Peter Such and Richard Rabone. Oxford: Oxbow, 2009.
Breviarium apostolorum ex nomine vel locis ubi praedicaverunt orti vel obiti sunt. 7th century. Bibliotheca Hagiographica Latina, manuscript 652.
La Chanson de Roland: The Song of Roland, The French Corpus. Edited by Joseph J. Duggan. Turnhout: Brepols, 2006.
Châtillon, Gautier de. *Alexandreis*. Accessed November 20, 2018. https://www.hs-augsburg.de/~harsch/Chronologia/Lspost12/Gualterus/gua_al00.html.
Chazan, Robert. *Reassessing Jewish Life in Medieval Europe*. New York: Cambridge University Press, 2010.
Cluny, Bernard of. *Scorn for the World: Bernard of Cluny's De contemptu mundi*. Translated by Ronald E. Pepin. East Lansing: Colleagues, 1991.
Connolly, Jane E. *Translation and Poetization in the Quaderna Vía. Study and Edition of the "Libro de miseria d'omne"*. Madison: Hispanic Seminary of Medieval Studies, 1987.
Concordia de Antealtares. 1435. Universidad de Santiago de Compostela.
Cuesta Serrano, Jaime. Introduction to *Libro de miseria de omne*, 11–79. Edited by Jaime Cuesta Serrano. Madrid: Cátedra, 2012.
Delaruelle, E. "The Crusading Idea in Cluniac Literature of the Eleventh Century." In *Cluniac Monasticism in the Central Middle Ages*, edited by Noreen Hunt. 191–216. Hamden: Archon, 1971.
Donovan, Richard B. *The Liturgical Drama in Medieval Spain*. Toronto: Pontifical Institute of Mediaeval Studies, 1958.
Dutton, Brian. "French Influences in the Spanish Mester de Clerecía." In *Medieval Studies in Honor of Robert White Linker*, edited by Brian Dutton, J. Woodrow Hassell, Jr., and John E. Keller, 73–93. Madrid: Castalia, 1973.

Evans, Joan. *Monastic Life at Cluny, 910-1157*. Hamden: Archon, 1968.
Gaunt, Simon. "Travel and Orientalism." In *The Cambridge History of French Literature*, edited by William Burgwinkle, Nicholas Hammond, and Emma Wilson, 121-30. Cambridge: Cambridge University Press, 2011.
Haskins, Charles Homer. *The Renaissance of the 12th Century*. Cambridge, MA: Harvard University Press, 1971.
The Holy Rule of Saint Benedict. Accessed November 20, 2018. https://christdesert.org/prayer/rule-of-st-benedict/.
Hirsau, Conrad de. *Dialogus super auctores*. Edited by Robert B. C. Huygens. Leiden: Brill, 1970.
Hunt, Noreen. *Cluny Under Saint Hugh, 1049-1109*. Notre Dame: University of Notre Dame Press, 1968.
Kaplan, Gregory. *El culto a San Millán en Valderredible: Las Iglesias rupestres y la formación del Camino de Santiago*. Santander: Goberno de Cantabria, 2007.
Lapesa, Rafael. "La apócope de la vocal en castellano antiguo: intento de explicación histórica." In *Estudios dedicados a Menéndez Pidal*, 2:185-226. 7 vols. in 8. Madrid: Consejo Superior de Investigaciones Científicas, 1950-62.
Latini, Brunetto. *Li Livres dou Trésor*. Ca. 1315-1325. British Library, Yates Thompson, manuscript 19.
Liber Sancti Jacobi: Codex Calixtinus. Translated (from Latin to Spanish) by A. Moralejo, C. Torres, and J. Feo. La Coruña: Xunta de Galicia, Consellería de Cultura, Comunicación Social e Turismo, 1998.
Libro de Alexandre. Edited by Jesús Cañas. 3rd ed. Madrid: Cátedra, 2000.
Libro de miseria de omne. Edited by Jaime Cuesta Serrano. Madrid: Cátedra, 2012.
López Alsina, Fernando. "Concordia de Antealtares." In *Santiago, camino de Europa: Culto y cultura en la peregrinación a Santiago de Compostela*, edited by Serafín Moralejo Álvarez, and Fernando López Alsina, 250-51. Santiago de Compostela: Fundación Caja de Madrid, 1993.
Manuscript M-77. 13th-19th century. Biblioteca Menéndez Pelayo. Santander, Spain.
Manuscritos de Valderredible. Edited by Julián Berzosa Guerrero. Polientes: Ayuntamiento de Valderredible, 2017.
Marcou, P. B. "The Origins of the Rule Forbidding Hiatus in French Verse." *Publications of the Modern Language Association* 11, no. 3 (1896): 331-35.
Melville, Gert. *The World of Medieval Monasticism: Its History and Forms of Life*. Translated by James D. Mixson. Collegeville: Liturgical Press, 2016.
Meun, Jean de (and Guillaume de Lorris). *Roman de la Rose*. Edited by André Mary. Paris: Gallimard, 2006.
Michael, Ian. *The Treatment of Classical Material in the "Libro de Alexandre"*. Manchester: Manchester University Press, 1970
Navascués, Joaquín María de. "La dedicación de la iglesia de Santa María y de todas las Vírgenes de Mérida." *Archivo español de Arqueología* 21 (1948): 309-53.
Peña de San José, Joaquín. "Documentos del convento de San Millán de la Cogolla en los que figura don Gonzalo de Berceo." *Berceo* 50 (1959): 79-93.
Pérez Celada, Julio A. *Documentación del monasterio de San Zoilo de Carrión (1047-1300)*. Palencia: Garrido Garrido, 1986.
Pérez de Urbel, Justo. "Orígenes del culto de Santiago en España." *Hispania Sacra* 5 (1952): 1-31.
Petrucci, Armando. *Historia de la escritura e historia de la Sociedad*. Valencia: Seminari d'estudis sobre la cultura escrita, 1999.
Pont-Sainte-Maxence, Guernes de. *Vie de Saint Thomas le Martyr*. Lund: Gleerup, 1922.

Quain, Edwin. A. "The Medieval Accessus Ad Auctores." *Traditio* 3 (1945): 215–64.
Ramón Royo, Juan. "Las reliquias viajeras." In *Las reliquias y sus cultos*, edited by Francisco José Alfaro Pérez and Carolina Naya Franco, 33–58. Zaragoza: Universidad de Zaragoza, 2018.
Riché, Pierre. *Education and Culture in the Barbarian West, Sixth through Eighth Centuries.* Translated by John J. Contreni. Columbia: University of South Carolina Press, 1976.
Rickard, Peter. *A History of the French Language.* 2nd ed. London: Unwin Hyman, 1989.
Rico, Francisco. "La clerecía del mester." *Hispanic Review* 53 (1985): 1–23.
Royo, Juan Ramón. "Las reliquias viajeras." In *Las reliquias y sus cultos*, edited by Francisco José Alfaro Pérez and Carolina Naya Franco, 33–58. Zaragoza: Universidad de Zaragoza, 2018.
Ruiz, Juan. *The Book of Good Love.* Translated by Elizabeth Drayson Macdonald. London: Everyman, 1999.
——. *Libro de buen amor.* Edited by Alberto Blecua. Madrid: Cátedra, 1992.
Shaver-Crandell, Annie and Paula Gerson. *The Pilgrim's Guide to Santiago de Compostela: A Gazetteer.* Turnhout: Harvey Miller, 1995.
Soifer Irish, Maya. *Jews and Christians in Medieval Castile: Tradition, Coexistence, and Change.* Washington, DC: The Catholic University of America Press, 2016.
Stones, Alison. "Notes on Three Illuminated Alexander Manuscripts." In *The Medieval Alexander Legend and Romance Epic*, edited by Peter Noble, Lucie Polak, and Claire Isoz, 193–241. Millwood: Kraus, 1982.
Such, Peter and Richard Rabone. Introduction to *Book of Alexander (Libro de Alexandre)*, 1–82. Translated by Peter Such and Richard Rabone. Oxford: Oxbow, 2009.
Tors, Lambert li. *Li Romans d'Alixandre.* Edited by Heinrich Michelant. Stuttgart: Litterarische Verein, 1846.
Uría Maqua, Isabel. *Panorama crítico del "mester de clerecía".* Madrid: Castalia, 2000.
Verbiginale. Ca. 1200–1299. Biblioteca Nacional de España, manuscript 1578. Accessed November 20. 2018. http://bdh.bne.es/bnesearch/biblioteca/Verbiginale%20%20%20%20/qls/bdh0000008324;jsessionid=BDDE8BB136FDA448DC29C54BB7C7669E.
La Vie de Saint Alexis. Edited by T. D. Hemming. Exeter: University of Exeter Press, 1994.

Chapter 2

EARLY JEWISH *CUADERNA VÍA* POETRY

DURING THE THIRTEENTH century, contact between Christians and Jews was encouraged by the fact that monasteries could at times be public spaces. One space that functioned as such was the cloister, where academic lessons were typically imparted and which also functioned as a central meeting place. Such was the case at St. Martin of Tournai, where, in addition to the "activities of the cathedral school":

> There was also a constant procession through the cloister of laymen from various walks of life. Some were workmen and provisioners, others were bringing their children to the school or collecting them, and still others were the friends and relatives of the canons themselves [...]. The townsfolk too often used the cloister for meetings of the town council or municipal court, and many no doubt wandered in and out waiting for their meetings to begin.[1]

As mentioned in chapter 1, at Cluny the cloister functioned as a place where monks engaged in reading, and it would be logical to conclude that this is where they read (and perhaps heard readings of) manuscripts from which they learned the techniques of *cuaderna vía* poetry. Public recitation of *cuaderna vía* poems outside of monasteries enhanced the possibility for contact between Christian clerics and Jews because Jewish communities were located nearby important Castilian pilgrimage monasteries and at times under their control. For example, in 1221 King Fernando III (r. 1217–1252) decreed that Jews living on lands in Burgos controlled by Santa María de las Huelgas were to be vassals of that monastery.[2] Other monasteries situated close to Jewish communities include San Zoilo in Carrión de los Condes, which will be discussed in the following chapter, and the monastery in Frómista (which included the Church of San Martín) annexed to San Zoilo.

Interaction between Jews and Christian clerics was also an offshoot of the fact that commercial transactions between monasteries and Jews were a part of daily life on the Camino de Santiago. Commerce grew in response to increased pilgrim traffic during the

---

1 *The Restoration of the Monastery of Saint Martin of Tournai*, trans. Nelson, 140–41.
2 Soifer Irish, *Jews and Christians in Medieval Castile*, 97.

ABSTRACT The poems analysed in the present volume demonstrate that some Christian clerics collaborated with Jews in Castilian monasteries on the Camino de Santiago. These poems, as I demonstrate in the cases of anonymous works in chapter 2, "Early Jewish *Cuaderna Vía* Poetry," reveal that during the thirteenth century Jews began to compose *cuaderna vía* poetry, which could only have occurred through study in monastic schools with Christian clerics, who were conduits of written culture and the only individuals capable of instructing others in this verse form. Jews living close to Castilian pilgrimage monasteries would have been aware that *cuaderna vía* poetry was recited publicly, and this motivated their interest in exploiting that medium. The fact that Jewish *cuaderna vía* poems appear in medieval and early-modern Jewish prayer books reveals why some Jews learned to compose a type of verse that was only taught in monastic schools, that is, in order to produce liturgical texts that could be recited aloud.

twelfth century. As monasteries (and cathedrals) expanded in the hopes of attracting more pilgrims, nearby lands were often purchased from Jews. Maya Soifer Irish underscores the fact that, in land transactions of the period by Cathedrals and monasteries, "Jews almost inevitably appear as the sellers of property, while the religious institutions and individual clerics are overwhelmingly the buyers."[3] Over time, Jews "reappear in a limited number of sources as tenants of monasteries" and it became common for "Jewish and Moorish artisans to labor in workshops that belonged to religious institutions," which are historically documented instances of an interconfessional coexistence on the Camino.[4] Physical proximity and economic transactions between monasteries and Jewish communities undoubtedly contributed to interaction within monastic schools, where Jews learned the *cuaderna vía* norms that enabled them to compose poems in Castilian. Although the identities of these Jewish poets are unknown, their works speak to a formation in the same type of high-culture Christian poetry.

One example is "El Dio alto que los çielos sostiene" (Lofty God who sustains the heavens), which consists of fifty-one verses that are distributed, according to their rhyme pattern, among ten quatrains, three tercets, and one couplet, with the use of quatrains and a clear tendency toward consonant rhyme linking the poem to the Christian clerical *cuaderna vía* tradition[5]:

1. Lofty God who sustains the heavens,
   and from whom even water and fire comes,
   and who keeps the land above the water,
   governor who maintains the living.

2. His name has been placed in the Law
   to give it to His chosen people.

3. They blessed His name all together,
   the newborn and the young children,
   and they said: "He is lightning and thunder
   and He controls the sun, the stars and the moon.

4. After God created Adam,
   he was sleeping peacefully,
   and woman was taken from his side
   to serve him and obey his commands.

5. When Adam was keeping his garden,
   which he kept up well,
   the serpent entered through the gate,
   and spoke into the woman's ear.

6. He said to her: "Woman, come with me
   to a tree that bears many delicious figs;
   we will eat and you will be my friend,
   and you will know the taste of wheat bread."

---

3 Soifer Irish, *Jews and Christians in Medieval Castile*, 90.

4 Soifer Irish, *Jews and Christians in Medieval Castile*, 91 and 93, respectively.

5 Full consonant rhyme is achieved in most of the quatrains in "El Dio alto que los çielos sostiene" according to the following scheme: -iene, -ido, -una, -ado, -aua, -igo, -ado, [...], -ientes, -ero.

7. After they had filled up on figs,
   and she had given a fig to her husband,
   who had never had such a terrible snack.

8. After their eyes were opened,
   they saw their nakedness;
   they covered themselves with [...] leaves
   and hid in fear behind a tree.

9. Later on, the God of the heavens uttered a great cry:
   "Where are you, Adam? Where are you hiding?
   If you have eaten from the Tree of Wisdom
   By My name, it will cost you dearly."

10. He said: "Oh Lord, I was born unlucky!
    The woman you gave me has sold me out;
    she was the one who gave me a fig,
    I have no idea whether it was from the prohibited tree."

11. Because she was in a tough spot,
    the woman spoke freely:
    "Oh Lord, the serpent doomed me,
    because you made me from a rib from only one side!"

12. Later on, God convened his court,
    and the serpent was eternally cursed,
    and the woman was given the pain of labor,
    and the man was given a great desire to be dead.

13. Because of this evil, we all seem to lie,
    through the figs that we eat with our teeth;
    we all will die, as all living beings do.

14. Cursed were our forefathers,
    who believed in wooden idols
    and who did not believe in the true Lord.[6]

---

6 1. "El Dio alto que los çielos sostiene / e avn el agua con el fuego aviene / e la tierra sobre el agua detiene, gouernador que a los biuos mantiene, / 2. el su nonbre en la ley lo a metido / para darlo al su pueblo escogido. / 3. Bendixeran el su nonbre a vna / los nasçidos e ninnos de la cuna, / e dixeron: 'Éste relanpa e truna / e saca sol e estrellas e luna.' / 4. Quando el Dio Adán ovo criado, / él se estaua durmiendo asosegado, / e a la muger sacó del su costado / para seruirlo e fazer su mandado. / 5. Quando Adán en el huerto se estaua / guardándolo, e bien se lo labraua, / el culebro por la puerta entraua; / a la muger al oydo le fablaua. / 6. Díxole asy: 'Muger, vete comigo / a vn árbol donde ay tanto buen figo: / comeremos e averme as por amigo, / e saberás quál es el pan de trigo.' / 7. Desque de los figos se oviera fartado, / al marido vn figo le avía dado: / nunca Adam comió tan mal bocado. / 8. Desque sus ojos ovieran abiertos, / sus vergüenças de fuera se las vieron: / con fojas [...] se las cubrieron / e tras vn árbol con temor se ascondieron. / 9. Luego el Dio del çielo dio vn grand grito: / '¿Dónde estás, Adán? ¿Dónde te as ascondido? / Sy del árbol del saber as comido, / ¡por el mi nonbre, caro será vendido!' / 10. Dixo: '¡Ay, Sennor! ¡Por malo fue [sic] nasçido! / La muger que me distes me ay vendido: / de su mano dado me avía vn figo, / no sé sy era del árbol defendido.' / 11. Commo la muger se viera en fuerte presa, / ally fabló con su lengua suelta: / '¡Ay, Sennor! ¡El culebro me ay muerta, / pues tú me feziste de vna costilla tuerta!' / 12. Luego el Dio mandó juntar sus cortes; / al culebro maldíxole las sortes, / e a la muger parir con dolor forte, / e al onbre dio grand lazario [sic] de morte. / 13. Por este mal todos paremos mientes.

"El Dio alto que los çielos sostiene" was first brought to light in 1960 by María del Carmen Pescador, who published a transcription (with modernized punctuation and accent marks) of the only textual witness to the poem, from which all quotations derive in the present study. The manuscript of two folios, housed in the Archivo Histórico Nacional de España, also contains two other previously unknown poems: "A los que adoran en la vera cruz" (To those who worship the true cross), and "Remiénbrense vuestros entendimientos" (Recall what you have learned).[7]

Pescador's palaeographic analysis of this manuscript reveals that it dates from the late fourteenth or early fifteenth centuries.[8] However, there are indications within the text of "El Dio alto que los çielos sostiene" that suggest that it was composed prior to that time. One example is the use of the masculine noun "culebro," or "snake," rather than the feminine "culebra" as in modern Castilian. The use of the masculine form in verses 5c ("el culebro"), 11c ("El culebro"), and 12b ("al culebro") recalls the masculine form used in early thirteenth-century Castilian works such as *La fazienda de ultra mar*.[9] A thirteenth-century date for the manuscript is also a possibility in light of a feature of the script employed—"redonda libraria" (Spanish round hand)—namely, the joining of letters with a continuous stroke of the quill. Pescador observes this feature in manuscripts composed in Spanish round hand during the second half of the thirteenth century.[10] In fact, this feature is found in manuscripts composed in Spanish round hand as early as 1218 and, as confirmed by Ángel Canellas and Albert Derolez,[11] was widely employed by Spanish and Portuguese scribes from that time until the early fifteenth century.

While it is difficult to date the only textual witness to "El Dio alto que los çielos sostiene," there are elements of the poem that point toward Jewish authorship, including the use of the form "Dio" (v. 1a, 4a, 9a, 12a) to name "God" rather than the Christian form "Dios."[12] The use as source material of the Midrash, a medieval compilation of rabbinic exegetical interpretations, may not only indicate that the poet was Jewish but also that this individual possessed a formal religious education. Díaz-Más identifies a midrashic source in the classification of the forbidden fruit in "El Dio alto que los çielos sostiene" as

---

/ Por los figos que comimos por los dientes / todos morremos; asy farán los biuientes. / 14. Maldito fue el linnaje primero, / que creyeron en ydolos de madero / e descreyeron del Sennor verdadero" (Pescador, "Tres nuevos poemas medievales," 242–44).

7 As Pescador explains in her study ("Tres nuevos poemas medievales," 242), she came across the manuscript, which was uncatalogued and not accompanied by any information regarding its provenance, by chance while looking through a stack of papers. The manuscript is currently catalogued as Archivo Histórico Nacional de España, Miscelánea cajón 12 (BETA manid 1195).

8 Pescador, "Tres nuevos poemas medievales," 247–49.

9 *La fazienda de ultra mar*, ed. Lazar (63, 88).

10 Pescador, "Tres nuevos poemas medievales," 247.

11 Canellas, *Exempla scripturarum latinarum*, 85–87, and Albert Derolez, *The Palaeography of Gothic Manuscript Books*, 113–14.

12 About the form "Dio," Lapesa writes: "Los judíos españoles decían *el Dio* en lugar de *Dios*, que les parecía un plural adecuado al trinitarismo cristiano" (*Historia de la lengua española*, 525–26). The Spanish Jews said *el Dio* instead of *Dios*, which seemed to them a plural form that expressed Christian Trinitarianism.

a fig (v. 6b, 7a, 7b, 10c), which is based on a rabbinic interpretation of the episode of the fall of Adam and Eve in Genesis [13]:

> Adam tried to gather leaves from the trees to cover part of their bodies, but he heard one tree after the other say: "There is the thief that deceived his Creator. Nay, the foot of pride shall not come against me, nor the hand of the wicked touch me. Hence, and take no leaves from me!" Only the fig-tree granted him permission to take of its leaves. That was because the fig was the forbidden fruit itself. Adam had the same experience as that prince who seduced one of the maid-servants in the palace. When the king, his father, chased him out, he vainly sought a refuge with the other maid-servants, but only she who had caused his disgrace would grant him assistance.[14]

This midrashic source is not the only rabbinic influence on the poem. Another tale was also consulted by the author of "El Dio alto que los çielos sostiene" during the composition of the sixth quatrain:

> He said to her: "Woman, come with me
> to a tree that bears many delicious figs:
> we will eat and you will be my friend,
> and you will know the taste of wheat bread."

The allusion to "pan de trigo" (wheat bread) in v. 6d involves a "[p]urely midrashic" tradition according to which the "forbidden fruit is identified [...] [with] wheat (which grew on stalks as tall as the cedars of Lebanon)."[15] The poet's knowledge of the Midrash points to his formal training in Jewish religious texts.

The verse lengths in "El Dio alto que los çielos sostiene" also point to its Jewish provenance. Paloma Díaz-Mas concludes that "the verses tend to be dodecasyllabic and they are grouped in monorhymed quatrains," and she attributes any deterioration to "a process of transmission that was not only written, but oral."[16] Such deterioration is evident in the cases of a verbal concordance error in v. 10a ("fue" [he was] instead of "fui" [I was]) and omitted terms in v. 8c, which, as Pescador explains, is too short and probably lacks the complete phrase "con fojas de figuera" (with fig leaves), whose inclusion would increase the syllable count in the verse from eight to twelve.[17] A similar example is found in v. 11b, the shortest verse in the poem with ten syllables, which may indicate that a word was lost during transmission. At the same time, the appearance of different verse lengths in "El Dio alto que los çielos sostiene" may reveal that the author had not yet mastered all of the norms of Castilian *cuaderna vía* versification, in particular with respect to hiatus and synalepha.

---

13 Díaz-Más, "Un género casi perdido," 335.

14 Ginzberg, *The Legends of the Jews*, 1:75.

15 Ginzberg, *The Legends of the Jews*, 5:97n70.

16 "los versos tienden a ser dodecasílabos y a agruparse en tetrástrofos monorrimos"; "un proceso de transmisión no sólo escrita, sino también oral" (Díaz-Más, "Un género casi perdido," 334).

17 Pescador, "Tres nuevos poemas medievales," 243n4. The phrase "con fojas de figuera" probably formed part of the original version of the poem insofar as it corresponds to a phrase from Genesis 3:7 in late medieval Castilian renditions of the Old Testament such as *Escorial Bible I.j.4* (57).

Insofar as the extent to which synalepha is used is difficult to determine, a more accurate determination of the verse lengths in "El Dio alto que los çielos sostiene" is achieved by only considering verses in which no contact between word-final and word-initial vowels occurs. There are fourteen such verses in "El Dio alto que los çielos sostiene," with seven being hendecasyllabic (v. 3b, 6d, 8a, 8b, 9c, 12b, 13a), five being dodecasyllabic (v. 5d, 9d, 13b, 14b, 14c), and with one verse of thirteen syllables (v. 13c), and another of ten (v. 11b). While this distribution does not directly confirm Díaz-Mas's aforementioned conclusion that "the verses tend to be dodecasyllabic," when the phrase "de figuera" (with fig [leaves]) is added to v. 8c, the syllabic count rises from eight to twelve, which results in six dodecasyllabic verses (v. 5d, 8c, 9d, 13b, 14b, 14c), a number that stands out in light of a similar tendency toward dodecasyllabic verses in other early Jewish *cuaderna vía* poems.[18]

Another poem that displays this tendency is "Cuando el rey Nimrod al campo saldriya" ("When King Nimrod was in the field"), which has been preserved orally and in several manuscripts in Hebrew *aljamiado*, that is, medieval Castilian words written (or, more precisely, phonetically transcribed) in Hebrew characters:

1. When King Nimrod was in the field
   he was looking at the stars in the heavens,
   and he saw a holy light in the Jewish quarter
   because Abraham our father would be born.

2. Afterwards he entrusted all the midwives
   with killing all women who became pregnant
   and gave birth to sons,
   because Abraham our father would be born.

3. Terah's wife became pregnant,
   and each day they asked her:
   "Why do you look so uneasy?"
   She already knew the misfortune that awaited.

4. After nine months she was ready to give birth,
   and she walked through the fields and vineyards
   so she would not be discovered by her husband,
   and she found a cave where she gave birth to him.

5. At that time he spoke to her:
   "Mother, let us leave this cave,
   because I already have someone who will suckle me,
   since I am the servant of the true Lord."

6. After twenty days she went to visit him,
   and she saw the child jump up and down,
   while staring straight into the heavens
   to know the true God.

7. "Mother, my mother, what are you looking for here?"
   "A cherished son who I left here,
   and I came to see if he is still here.
   If he is alive I will be consoled."

---

18 For example, "por-el-mi-non-bre-ca-ro-se-rá-ven-di-do" (v. 9d).

8. "Mother, my mother, what are you saying?
   How could you leave a cherished son?
   Why are you coming to visit him after twenty days?
   I am your son, the servant of God."

9. At nightfall I looked at the moon,
   and I counted the stars one by one.
   At dawn I saw that they were covered up,
   and I said: "This is not the true God."

10. I saw the sun lighting up the sky,
    and in my heart I thought it was God.
    I saw dusk set in,
    and I said: "This is not the true God."

11. See, my mother, that God is one,
    and he created the heavens one by one.
    Tell Nimrod that he lost his nerve
    because he refuses to believe in the true one.

12. The news of this reached Nimrod,
    who ordered that he be brought to him as quickly as possible:
    "Before he denies everything else,
    and everyone abandons me and believes in the true one."

13. They humiliated me greatly in bringing me here;
    Then [Abraham] pulled [Nimrod] up from his seat:
    "Why do you consider yourself to be a god, wicked Nimrod?
    Why do you not believe in the true one?"

14. "Light up an oven and make it hot,
    tie him up with ropes, because he understands,
    throw him in with his guiles, because he knows too much.
    If God sets him free, He is the true one."

15. He went walking into the oven,
    as if walking with angels,
    while the flames were white hot,
    and the true God set him free from there.

16. Abraham was a very pious man,
    and because of him we know the true God,
    and all who are born are pious,
    upon confirming the good deed of Abraham our father.

17. Let us now salute the birth of each man,
    may each one be born under a good sign.
    May Elijah the prophet appear to us
    and we will sing our praise to the true one.

18. Let us salute the godfather and the mohel,
    whose piety will bring the redeemer to us
    and have mercy on all of Israel.
    We will surely sing our praise to the true one.[19]

---

[19] The Castilian transcription is as follows: 1. Cuando el rey Nimrod al campo saldriya / miraba

The earliest manuscripts containing "Cuando el rey Nimrod al campo saldriya" date from the eighteenth century although, as I will explain below, the structure of the poem indicates that it was composed contemporary to "El Dio alto que los çielos sostiene." "Cuando el rey Nimrod al campo saldriya" depicts the foretelling by King Nimrod of the birth of Abraham and God's initial revelation to the future Patriarch, and the fact that the source is the Midrash again points to the author's formation in religious texts.[20] The poem condenses the narration of these events in a late medieval compilation of rabbinic interpretations, *Maaseh Avraham Avinu Alav Ha-Shalom* (The Deeds of Abraham our Father, May Peace Be with Him), which centres on the life of the patriarch Abraham.[21] The poet's portrayal of Nimrod as seeing "a holy light in the Jewish quarter / because Abraham our father would be born" while "looking at the stars in the heavens" parallels the beginning of the episode in *Maaseh Avraham Avinu*, in which Nimrod "was a cunning astrologer, who saw through the science of astrology that a man would be born in his day

---

en el cielo a la estrelleriya, / vido luz santa en el juderiya, / que habiya de nacer Abraham ʾābînû. / 2. Luego a las comadres encomendaba / que toda mujer que se encintara, / si pariya hijo, que lo matara, / que habiya de nacer Abraham abinu. / 3. La mujer de Térah quedó preñada, / de en diya en diya le demandaba: / "¿De qué tenés la cara tan demudada?" / Ella ya sabía el mal que teniya. / 4. A los mueve meses parir queriya, / se hue caminando por campos y viñas; / a su marido tal non descubririya, / topó una məʿārâ y lo paririya. / 5. Luego en aquella hora él le hablaba: / "Andávos la mi madre de la meará, / porque yo ya tengo a quen me alechará, / porque so criyado del Dio verdadero." / 6. A los vente diyas lo hue a visitar, / lo vido de enfrente mancebo saltar, / mirando en el cielo y bien atentar / para conocer al Dio de la verdad. / 7. "Madre, la mi madre, ¿qué buscas aquí?" / "Un hijo preciado que dejí aquí / lo vine a buscar si está por aquí; / si es que está vivo me consolo yo." / 8. "Madre, la mi madre, ¿qué hablas hablas?; / un hijo Preciado, ¿cómo lo dejas? / ¿Por qué a los vente diyas lo venís a visitar? / Yo so el vuestro hijo, criyado del Dio." / 9. Al anochecer vide a la luna, / contí a las estrellas una por una. / Al amanecer vide que se encubrió de una; / dije: "No es éste el Dio vedradero." / 10. Vide a el sol que se espandió, / pensí en mi corazón que era el Dio. / Vide a la tadre que se encubrió, / dije: "No es éste el Dio verdadero." / 11. Mirá la mi madre que el Dio es uno, / que criyó los cielos uno por uno. / Decílde a Nimrod que perdió su tino / porque no quere creer en el vedradero. / 12. Alcanzólo a saber el rey Nimrod esto, / mandó que lo traigan aína y presto: / "Antes que desniegue a todo el resto, / y dejen a mí y crean en el vedradero." / 13. Ya me lo trujeron con grande ʿelbôn; / trabólo de la silla con grande trabón: / "Por qué te tienes por Dio, tú, rāšāʿ Nimrod? / ¿Por qué non crees en el vedradero?" / 14. "¡Encendé un horno bien encendido!, / ¡ataldo con cuedras, porque es entendido!, / ¡aronjaldo con trabucos, porque es resabido!; / si Dio lo escapa es el vedradero." / 15. Entrando en el horno iba caminando, / con sus malʾākîm iba paseando, / y todos los leños fruto iban dando; / de allí lo escapó el Dio verdadero. / 16. Grande zehût tuvo el señor de Abraham, / que por él conocimos al Dio de la vedrad; / grande zejut tiene el señor parido, / que afirmó la miṣwâ de Abraham abinu. / 17. Saludemos ahora al señor parido, / que le sea besîmān ṭôb este nacido; / ʾēliyāhû hanābîʾ nos sea aparecido / y daremos loores al verdadero. 18. Saludemos al compadre y también al môhēl, que por su zejut nos venga el gôʾēl / y rîḥma a todo Yisrael. / Cierto loaremos al verdadero (Romero, *Coplas sefardíes*, 43–46). For a study of one of the manuscripts that contains "Cuando el rey Nimrod al campo saldriya," see *Judeo-Spanish Ballads from Bosnia*, ed. Armistead and Silverman, 13–29.

20 For depictions of the midrashic episodes and information on the sources, see Ginzberg, *The Legends of the Jews*, 1:186–93, 1:207–9; 5:212–13n34, 5:216–17n48.

21 The *Maaseh Avraham Avinu* was first published in 1580, in Constantinople. The work is thought to have been originally composed in Persia, where it was "written in Arabic" before being "translated into Hebrew" (Mehlman, "The *Maaseh Avraham Avinu*," 3).

and would arise against him, dissuade him of his faith, and defeat him."²² Moreover, in "Cuando el rey Nimrod al campo saldriya" the assignment of killing all pregnant women made by Nimrod to "all the midwives" is a summary of the midrashic version:

> [Nimrod] sent for his princes and governors and told them of the matter. He asked them, "What do you advise me to do about this child who is yet to be born?" They responded, "The counsel which we agree upon is that you should build a large house, set a guard at its entrance, then decree throughout your realm that all the pregnant women shall come there. After they arrive, they shall also bring the midwives so that they are with the pregnant women at the time of their delivery. Now when a woman's time to deliver arrives, the midwives will see, and if it is a boy, they will kill him at the womb, but if it is a girl they will let her live.²³

The next events in "Cuando el rey Nimrod al campo saldriya" also follow *Maaseh Avraham Avinu* closely, although the poem alters the midrashic portrayal of the abandonment of Abraham by his mother in the cave in which he is born (whereupon he is suckled by the archangel Gabriel before leaving the cave):

> Then she [Abraham's mother] opened her mouth and said, "I am the one who bore you at the time that king Nimrod killed seventy thousand male infants because of you. Now I greatly fear for you, for if he learns about your existence he will kill you! Therefore, it is better that you die in this cave so that my eyes do not see you slain upon my bosom." So she took her own clothing and swaddled him. Then she abandoned him in the cave and said, "May your God be with you. May God not fail you or forsake you [...]. God sent the angel Gabriel to sustain him and give him milk [...]. Then he [Abraham] began to walk about, left the cave [...]."²⁴

While Abraham's mother leaves her son to die according to *Maaseh Avraham Avinu*, in "Cuando el rey Nimrod al campo saldriya" it is not clear why twenty days pass before she "visit[s] him." However, it is apparent that the author of "Cuando el rey Nimrod al campo saldriya" knew the story from *Maaseh Avraham Avinu* insofar as in both renditions Abraham's mother does not recognize him upon returing to the cave because he has grown. In "Cuando el rey Nimrod al campo saldriya," Abraham's mother thus declares that she is looking for a "cherished son" without realizing that she is speaking to that individual, while in *Maaseh Avraham Avinu* she speaks to him although she does not "recognize him because he had grown greatly."²⁵ Of course, because "Cuando el rey Nimrod al campo saldriya" condenses *Maaseh Avraham Avinu*, a number of details are omitted in the poem, although additional parallels between the poetic and midrashic versions, such as the request of Abraham to his mother that she communicate to Nimrod that he is not a deity and the encounter between Abraham and Nimrod, again indicate the poet's thorough familiarity with his source.²⁶

---

22 Mehlman, "The *Maaseh Avraham Avinu*," 5 (the translation into English is by Mehlman).
23 Mehlman, "The *Maaseh Avraham Avinu*," 5–6 (the translation into English is by Mehlman).
24 Mehlman, "The *Maaseh Avraham Avinu*," 7–8 (the translation into English is by Mehlman).
25 Mehlman, "The *Maaseh Avraham Avinu*," 9 (the translation into English is by Mehlman).
26 Verses 11a–11d of "Cuando el rey Nimrod al campo saldriya," which describe Abraham's request, are based on the following passage from *Maaseh Avraham Avinu*: "He [Abraham] answered, 'Yes my

The climax of "Cuando el rey Nimrod al campo saldriya" occurs when Abraham's faith in God allows him to escape from a "white hot" oven, which takes place in *Maaseh Avraham Avinu* after an extended narration of Abraham's desecration and destruction of the idols in Nimrod's kingdom. Abraham is then thrown into prison in order that he starve to death, and he is again saved by God through the archangel Gabriel. Unlike the summarized episode in "Cuando el rey Nimrod al campo saldriya" in which Abraham is depicted as "walking into the oven, / as if walking with angels," in *Maaseh Avraham Avinu* several unsuccessful attempts are made at casting Abraham into the oven before he is ultimately catapulted into the flames, where Gabriel pays him another visit and God extinguishes the fire. Although Nimrod claims that Abraham has been saved by "Great sorcery!," his princes exclaim "No our lord, this is not sorcery!" and as the episode concludes they, along with all of Nimrod's subjects—in terms that recall the tone of the final three quatrains of "Cuando el rey Nimrod al campo saldriya"— announce their faith in "the God of Abraham."[27]

Insofar as the Midrash was only available in Hebrew in the Middle Ages, the author of "Cuando el rey Nimrod al campo saldriya" obviously knew that language, as did the author of "El Dio alto que los çielos sostiene." Further confirmation that the author of "Cuando el rey Nimrod al campo saldriya" was a speaker of Hebrew (and thus of Jewish provenance), is confirmed by the fact that the poem was written down in Hebrew characters, as well as by the inclusion of a number of Hebrew terms: "'ābînû" (אָבִינוּ [our father]); "məʿārâ" (מְעָרָה [cave]); "'elbôn" (עֶלְבּוֹן [humiliation]); "rāšāʿ" (רָשָׁע [wicked]); "mal'ākîm" (מַלְאָכִים [angels]); "zehût" (זְהוּת [which literally means "identity" but which is used in this context to communicate the notion of individual piety and worthiness for redemption]; "miṣwâ" (מִצְוָה [the performance of a divine commandment, or good deed]); "besîmān ṭôb" (בְּסִימָן טוֹב [under a good sign])[28]; "'ēliyāhû hanābî'" (אֵלִיָהוּ הַנָבִיא

---

mother, the God of heaven and the God of earth is also the God of Nimrod, son of Canaan. Now you to Nimrod and inform him of this" (Mehlman, "The *Maaseh Avraham Avinu*," 10 [the translation into English is by Mehlman]). Verse 13a alludes to the first attempt by Herod to arrest Abraham, which is thwarted by the archangel Gabriel according to *Maaseh Avraham Avinu*: "The Maggid said that the king ordered all the princes and all the warriors to come and take weapons from the royal arsenals. Thus they went forth to take Abraham. When Abraham our father saw that a great number of people were coming for him, trembling and great fear seized him on their account [...]. God heard his cry and saw his tears and sent the angel Gabriel to deliver him from their hand" (Mehlman, "The *Maaseh Avraham Avinu*," 11 [the translation into English is by Mehlman]). Verses 13b–13d, which describe the encounter between Abraham and Nimrod, are based on the following passage from *Maaseh Avraham Avinu*: "Abraham passed by the governors and prefects until he reached the royal throne, the one on which King Nimrod was seated. He grasped hold of the throne and shook it, proclaiming these words in a loud voice, 'O Nimrod, you loathsome man, who denies the unity of God, who does not believe in the living and ever-existent God [...]. Attest and declare as do I, that *Adonai* is God, God is unique and has no second, God has no body [...]. Further testify against yourself that you are a mortal [...].'" (Mehlman, "The *Maaseh Avraham Avinu*," 13–14 [the translation into English is by Mehlman]).

27 Mehlman, "The *Maaseh Avraham Avinu*," 22 (the translation into English is by Mehlman).
28 The phrase "besimán tov" continues to be used in the twenty-first century in Ladino to bless the birth of a newborn boy (Bunis, "Twenty-First-Century Talk about Judezmo," 350).

[Elijah the prophet]); "môhēl" (מוֹהֵל [circumciser]); "gô'ēl" (גוֹאֵל [redeemer]); and "rîḥma" (which is a variant of the Hebrew term for "mercy," רחמים [raḥămîm]).

The strophic form of "Cuando el rey Nimrod al campo saldriya" corresponds for the most part to the *zéjel*, a poetic genre of Islamic origin that became popular among medieval Spanish Jewish poets. The *zéjel* is characterized by the use of an *estribillo*, or refrain, which is repeated after tercets distinguished by their rhyme.[29] While a rhyming refrain typically repeats throughout a *zéjel*, in "Cuando el rey Nimrod al campo saldriya" the refrain varies in rhyme (-inu;-iya;-o;-ero), and the sixth quatrain is distinguished by its own rhyme (-a-). The appearance of this mono-rhymed quatrain indicates that the poet deviated from the *zéjel* tradition in order to imitate the type of stanza that exemplified *cuaderna vía* poetry. Further evidence of the poet's attempt to imitate *cuaderna vía* norms is the frequent employment of dodecasyllabic verses rather than the octosyllabic verses typically used in the *zéjel*.[30]

This frequency is evident in the twenty-one verses in "Cuando el rey Nimrod al campo saldriya" in which there is no contact between word-initial and word-final vowels. The syllabic count of these verses is as follows: eight dodecasyllabic verses (v. 3c, 4b, 4c, 5d, 6d, 7a, 8a, 8b), seven hendecasyllabic verses (v. 3a, 4a, 11b, 13d, 15b, 17d, 18d), five thirteen-syllable verses (v. 5b, 11d, 13b, 13c, 17b), and one fourteen-syllable alexandrine verse (16b). It is instructive to underscore that a dodecasyllabic count is achieved at times in "Cuando el rey Nimrod al campo saldriya" through the use of final acute terms—such as "aquí" ("here," v. 7a)—which brings the syllabic count to twelve according to Castilian norms of scansion. The dodecasyllabic verses in "Cuando el rey Nimrod al campo saldriya" thus reveal that the poet, who was accustomed to writing in Hebrew, had acquired a knowledge of stressed syllables in Castilian, in particular the difference between verses that carry the final stress on the penultimate syllable, such as "por-que-so-cri-ya-do-del-Dio-ver-da-de-ro" (v. 5d), and oxytonic verses that carry the final stress on the last syllable, such as verse 7a, to which a syllable is added so that it, like verse 5d, is dodecasyllabic ("Ma-dre-la-mi-ma-dre-qué-bus-cas-a-quí"+1).[31] The rhyme scheme in "Cuando el rey Nimrod al campo saldriya" also reveals a knowledge of Castilian *cuaderna vía* conventions regarding rhyme, in particular the use of consonant rhyme to indicate divisions between stanzas. At the same time, the presence of assonant rhyme—for example, between "encomendaba" ("entrusted," v. 2a) and "encintara" ("became pregnant," v. 2b)—may indicate that the poet had not yet acquired a mastery of Castilian consonant rhyme schemes.

The tendency toward dodecasyllabic verses in "Cuando el rey Nimrod al campo saldriya" recalls the same tendency in "El Dio alto que los çielos sostiene" and suggests that it is a thirteenth-century Jewish *cuaderna vía* poem. "Cuando el rey Nimrod al campo

---

[29] An example of a rhyme scheme of a *zéjel* is: bbba / ccca / [...] (with "a" representing the *estribillo*).

[30] On the frecuency of the octosyllabic verse in the *zéjel* tradition, see Domínguez Caparrós, *Métrica de Cervantes*, 116, and Menéndez Pidal, "Poesía arabe," 363.

[31] "since I am the servant of the true Lord'" (v. 5d); "'Mother, my mother, what are you looking for here?'" (v. 7a).

saldriya" is also an example of a Hebrew *aljamiado* poem in which the inclusion of a fourteen-syllable verse may reveal an attempt at achieving Castilian norms. The fact that these Hebrew *aljamiado* poems include verses ranging from ten to seventeen syllables, may be because their authors were far from mastering *cuaderna vía* techniques although such variation may also be due to centuries of oral transmission.

Another medieval Jewish *cuaderna vía* poem that demonstrates a tendency toward dodecasyllabic verses is "Cuando a Yerušaláyim vide en tanta fatiga" (When I saw Jerusalem in such dire straits) provides. This poem was first written down in Hebrew *aljamiado* during the late eighteenth century in Sarajevo:

1. When I saw Jerusalem in such dire straits,
   it made me think and I composed this song
   for Jerusalem, the friendly land.
   And we will sing our worship and praise.

2. Oh Jerusalem! The light of my eyes,
   with which we eliminate all hatred,
   and may our eyes see her splendour.

3. Oh Jerusalem! The fulfilled city
   that is loved by all the world.
   In her we will see our redemption fulfilled.

4. Oh Jerusalem! Esteemed city
   that is praised throughout the world.
   May we have the piety to see her fully built.

5. Oh Jerusalem! Cherished city
   that was cherished by the Lord of Moses,
   and that will be cherished in the hour of redemption.

6. And when people thought of her
   they left their palaces, possessions and vices behind,
   and they were unable to sleep.

7. And when they thought of her
   they remained awake,
   and sold their jewels out of love.

8. And when they see her in front of them
   she seems like the rising moon,
   and they leave their children and relatives.

9. And when they think of her from afar
   her bounty makes them lose interest in money,
   and forget about their possessions and all they have done.

10. Blessed are all who live in her
    and the sale of properties for her benefit,
    which brings good fortune to their souls.

11. I would be very pleased to live there.
    What a shame that we see that the Temple is destroyed!
    We beg God to see it rebuilt.

12. How should I praise you, light of the earth?
    All the nations try to be like her.
    Oh, Lord of the world, do not take us from you!

13. And her foods are very delicious;
    and her flowers are very glorious;
    even its weeds are very tasty.

14. And for the rich it is a very good land
    where they give charity
    so that their souls are free from all pain.

15. And for the poor it is a great place
    where they feel like the good rose,
    widows who live there are called fortunate

16. I love you dearly, my beloved land,
    and I beg of God for my wish to be fulfilled:
    that we will not be taken from her either in life or in death.[32]

As in the case of "Cuando el rey Nimrod al campo saldriya," the inclusion of Hebrew terms in "Cuando a Yerušaláyim vide en tanta fatiga" is indicative of its Jewish provenance. These terms include: "gə'ûlāh" (גְּאוּלָּה ["redemption"]; "zehût" (זְהוּת [piety]); and "ṣədāqâ" (צְדָקָה [charity]). "Cuando a Yerušaláyim vide en tanta fatiga" was found in a collection of *pizmonim*, that is, liturgical songs designed to accompany prayers or to be sung on religious festivals, which suggests that Jews imitated *cuaderna vía* norms in order to produce works that could be recited aloud. Indeed, the use of consonant rhyme in "Cuando a Yerušaláyim vide en tanta fatiga" (-iga, -ojos, -ida, [...]) was a *cuaderna vía* technique whose adoption would have facilitated the memorization of liturgical poems. As such, "Cuando a Yerušaláyim vide en tanta fatiga" centres on the theme of an apoca-

---

[32] The Castilian transcription is as follows: 1. Cuando a Yerušaláyim vide en tanta fatiga, / estuve pensando y hice esta cantiga / por Yerušaláyim la tiera amiga. / Y daremos loores y alabaciones. 2. ¡Ah Yerušaláyim!, la luz de mis ojos, / con ella quitamos todos los enojos / y la su grandeza vean nuestros ojos. / 3. ¡Ah Yerušaláyim!, la civdad cunplida / que de todo el mundo es mucho querida, / dientro de ella veremos la gə'ûlāh cunplida. / 4. ¡Ah Yerušaláyim!, civdad estimada / que por todo el mundo es mucho alabada, / tengamos zehût de verla fraguada. / 5. ¡Ah Yerušaláyim!, civdad deseada / que para el señor de Mosé fue muy deseada, / en hora de la regmición será mucho deseada. / 6. Y cuando la gente en ella pensaban / sarayes y mulkes y vicios dejaban, / el sueño del ojo se les tiraban. / 7. Y cuando en ell alas mientes metían / el sueño de los ojos se les quitarían; / por sus amores las joyas vendían. / 8. Y cuando ya la ven a ella de enfrente / parece la luna cuando está en creciente, / dejan a los hijos y a los parientes. / 9. Y cuando pensaban por ella de lejos / no contan moneda cuantos su provechos, / se olvidan sus bienes y todos sus hechos. 10. Beata a todos que en ella moraban / y a sus haciendas por ella gastaban, / hacen cavdal grande para sus almas. / 11. De morar en ella mucho me agrada. / ¡Guay que la vemos la Casa quemada!; / roguemos al Dio de verla fraguada. / 12. ¿Qué vos alabaré, lucia de las tieras? / Todas las naciones precuran por ella: / ¡ah, Señor del mundo, no mos quites de ella! / 13. Y las sus comidas son muy provechosas / y las sus flores son muy goloriosas, / hasta las yerbecicas son muy sabrosas. / 14. Y para los ricos es tiera muy buena / que hagan ṣədāqâ con las manos llenas, / escapan sus almas de todas las penas. / 15. Y para los pobres es muy buena cosa / que les yakisea como la buena rosa, / vivdas que moran en ella se llaman dichosas. / 16. Mucho vos estimo, mi tiera querida, / y yo del Dio demando demanda cunplida: / que no mos quites de ella ni en muerte ni en vida (Romero, *Coplas sefardíes*, 100–102).

lyptic Jewish return to Zion and the poet depicts a majestic Jerusalem where both rich and poor will live in harmony. While the strophic form follows the *zéjel* model of three rhymed verses with a repeating *estribillo* ("And we will sing our worship and praise"), a preponderance of dodecasyllabic (rather than octosyllabic) verses situates the composition of this poem contemporary to other early Jewish *cuaderna vía* works.[33]

Of the forty-eight verses in "Cuando a Yerušaláyim vide en tanta fatiga" (not including the *estribillo*, which remains constant throughout the poem), twenty-five do not involve contact between word-final and word-initial vowels (v. 2b, 2c, 3a, 4a, 4d, 5a, 6b, 7b, 9a, 9b, 10c, 11b, 11c, 12a, 12b, 13a, 13b, 13c, 14a, 14b, 14c, 15a, 15b, 15c, 16a). Of these 25 verses, seventeen are dodecasyllabic (v. 2b, 2c, 3a, 4a, 5a, 6b, 9a, 9b, 12a, 12b, 13a, 13c, 14a, 14b, 14c, 15a, 16a), five are hendecasyllabic (v. 4c, 10c, 11b, 11c, 13b), two have thirteen syllables (v. 7b, 15b), and one is a fourteen-syllable alexandrine verse (v. 15c). The tendency toward a dodecallylabic syllabic count is clearly evident in stanzas twelve, thirteen, and fourteen, in which seven of the nine verses have twelve syllables.[34]

The use of dodecasyllabic verses in Jewish *cuaderna vía* poems contrasts with the tendency in Christian *cuaderna vía* poems of the thirteenth century toward fourteen-syllable alexandrine verses. This contrast is the result of an acoustic phenomenon that, as Elena González-Blanco García explains, distinguishes syllabic counts in French and Spanish:

> Although at first it might seem surprising that a verse with two fewer syllables is given the same name as the Spanish alexandrine, this difference has a very simple metrical justification: syllabic counts in French include only those syllables located before the last accented vowel. For this reason, in the many cases when the last tonic vowel is followed by a syllable that contains a silent -e, this vowel is not pronounced, and thus is not counted for metrical purposes (which results in what is known as "feminine rhyme"). This same phenomenon occurs before the *medial caesura* that divides the alexandrine into two hemistiches; therefore, in metrical terms, in a dodecasyllabic verse with two silent syllables, one before the *caesura* and one at the end of the verse, the actual total would be 14 syllables, which is the equivalent of our [Spanish] alexandrine.[35]

---

33 The *estribillo*, "And we will sing our worship and praise" ("Y daremos loores y alabaciones") is repeated in an abbreviated form after most of the tercets.

34 For example, all three verses in stanza fourteen are dodecasyllabic: "Y-pa-ra-los-ri-cos-es-tie-ra-muy-bue-na / que-ha-gan-se-da-cá-con-las-ma-nos-lle-nas, / es-ca-pan-sus-al-mas-de-to-das-las-pe-nas."

35 "Aunque en un principio pudiera parecer sorpresivo el que se denominara con el mismo nombre a un verso con dos sílabas menos que el alejandrino español, dicha diferencia tiene una justificación métrica muy simple: el cómputo silábico en francés incluye solamente en su número de sílabas todas aquellas situadas antes de la última vocal acentuada, incluyendo a esta última. Por dicha razón, en muchos de los casos, cuando a la última tónica sigue una sílaba que contiene un -*e* muda, ésta no se pronuncia, por lo que tampoco computa a efectos métricos (hecho conocido como la rima femenina). Este mismo fenómeno se produce ante la cesura medial que divide el alejandrino en dos hemistiquios, por lo tanto, en un verso dodecasílabo a efectos métricos que tuviera dos sílabas mudas antes de la cesura y al final del verso, el resultado serían, efectivamente, 14 sílabas en su totalidad y equivalente, por tanto, a nuestro alejandrino" (González-Blanco García, "Las raíces del 'mester de clerecía,'" 197n5).

From a Castilian perspective, twelve-syllable Old French alexandrine verses that contain two instances of word-final -e, appear to contain fourteen syllables (that is, if word-final -e is counted). This is illustrated by verses such as the following one from Lambert's Alexander poem (in which there is no contact between word-final and word-initial vowels): "et conquerre par force les castiaus et les tors" ("and conquering them by force").[36] Whereas there are fourteen syllables according to a Castilian syllabic computation of this verse (et-con-que-rre-par-for-ce-les-cas-ti-aus-et-les-tors), there are only twelve in the Old French syllabic count because the two instances of word final -e are not included (et-con-querre-par-force-les-cas-ti-aus-et-les-tors). When they consulted manuscripts containing French poems as part of their monastic training, Castilian clerics no doubt perceived instances of word-final -e as components of syllables that they naturally pronounced in their native language. The number of syllables in the Spanish alexandrine thus increased from twelve to fourteen.

While Christians and Jews both grouped their alexandrine verses in quatrains with consonant rhyme, Jewish *cuaderna vía* poetry reveals that Jews imitated the French style by composing dodecasyllabic alexandrines. The reason for this is that they were accustomed to writing in Hebrew and may not have had a firm grasp of Castilian norms. Jewish poets therefore incorporated French acoustic norms when composing verses in Castilian or Hebrew *aljamiado*, which is the reason they produced twelve-syllable alexandrines. At the same time, the appearance of some fourteen-syllable alexandrines in Jewish poems demonstrates sporadic success in achieving Castilian *cuaderna vía* norms and, by extension, suggests that Jewish *cuaderna vía* poetry was evolving during the thirteenth century. This evolution is most clearly revealed in Jewish *cuaderna vía* poems composed during the fourteenth century, which will be considered in the following chapters.

---

36 Tors, 7 (v. 19).

Works Cited

Bunis, David M. "Twenty-First-Century Talk about Judezmo on the Ladinokomunita Website." In *Languages of Modern Jewish Cultures: Comparative Perspectives*, edited by Joshua Miller and Anita Norich, 321–60. Ann Arbor: University of Michigan Press, 2016.

Canellas, Ángel. *Exempla scripturarum latinarum in usum scholarum*. 2 vols. Zaragoza: Librería General, 1966–67.

Derolez, Albert. *The Palaeography of Gothic Manuscript Books: From the Twelfth to the Early Sixteenth Century*. Cambridge: Cambridge University Press, 2003.

Díaz-Mas, Paloma. "Un género casi perdido de la poesía castellana medieval: La clerecía rabínica." *Boletín de la Real Academia Española* 73 (1993): 329–46.

Domínguez Caparrós, José. *Métrica de Cervantes*. Alcalá de Henares: Centro de Estudios Cervantinos, 2002.

Escorial Bible I.j.4. Edited by O. H. Hauptmann. Philadelphia: University of Pennsylvania Press, 1953.

La fazienda de ultra mar. Edited by Moshé Lazar. Salamanca: Universidad de Salamanca, 1965.

Ginzberg, Louis. *The Legends of the Jews*. 7 vols. Philadelphia: Jewish Publication Society, 1968.

González-Blanco García, Elena. "Las raíces del 'mester de clerecía'." *Revista de Filología Española* 88 (2008): 195–207.

Judeo-Spanish Ballads from Bosnia. Edited by Samuel G. Armistead and Joseph H. Silverman. Philadelphia: University of Pennsylvania Press, 1971.

Lapesa, Rafael. *Historia de la lengua española*. 9th ed. Madrid: Gredos, 1988.

Maaseh Avraham Avinu Alav Ha-Shalom. In *Bet HaMidrasch*, 25–34, edited by Adolph Jellinek. Jerusalem: Wahrmann, 1967.

Manuscript Miscelánea cajón 12 (BETA manid 1195). 14th–15th century. Archivo Histórico Nacional de España. Madrid, Spain.

Mehlman, Bernard H. "The *Maaseh Avraham Avinu Alav Ha-Shalom*: Translation, Notes, and Commentary." *CCAR Journal: The Reform Jewish Quarterly* (spring 2012): 1–28.

Menéndez Pidal, Ramón. "Poesía árabe y poesía europea." *Bulletin Hispanique* 40, no. 4 (1938): 337–423.

Pescador, María del Carmen. "Tres nuevos poemas medievales." *Nueva Revista de Filología Hispánica* 14 (1960): 242–50.

The Restoration of the Monastery of Saint Martin of Tournai. By Herman of Tournai. Translated by Lynn H. Nelson. Washington, DC: Catholic University of America Press, 1996.

Romero, Elena, ed. *Coplas sefardíes: Primera selección*. Córdoba: El Almendro, 1988.

Soifer Irish, Maya. *Jews and Christians in Medieval Castile: Tradition, Coexistence, and Change*. Washington, DC: The Catholic University of America Press, 2016.

Tors, Lambert li. *Li Romans d'Alixandre*. Edited by Heinrich Michelant. Stuttgart: Litterarischer Verein, 1846.

Chapter 3

SEM TOB'S *PROVERBIOS MORALES*: THE EPITOME OF JEWISH *CUADERNA VÍA* POETRY[1]

THE JEWISH POET who assimilated Christian norms with the greatest precision was Sem Tob Ibn Ardutiel ben Isaac—better known as Sem Tob de Carrión—who composed his only Castilian *cuaderna vía* poem, *Proverbios morales* (Moral Proverbs), in the early 1350s.[2] Sem Tob offers a wealth of guidance in *Proverbios morales*, whose 725 stanzas comprise almost entirely two fourteen-syllable alexandrine verses divided into two seven-syllable hemistiches.[3] Sem Tob lived in the town of Carrión de los Condes, whose ten thousand inhabitants during the fourteenth century included between three hundred and six hundred Jewish families.[4] Jews had been granted the right to reside in Carrión de los Condes in a royal charter issued during the late eleventh century, and documents reveal that Jews lived in communities situated next to several pilgrimage churches in Carrión de los Condes, including the Benedictine monastery of San Zoilo.[5]

---

[1] An earlier version of this chapter was published as "Sem Tob's *Provervios morales*: A Rabbinic Voice for Anti-Rabbinic Sectarianism" in *Enarratio: Publications of the Medieval Association of the Midwest* 21 (2017): 18–35. Accessed November 20, 2018. https://kb.osu.edu/handle/1811/60329.

[2] Sem Tob's allusion in *Proverbios morales* (v. 3a) to the death of King Alfonso XI sets a *terminus a quo* for its composition of March 26, 1350.

[3] The exceptions, stanzas 34 to 39, are quatrains which comprise heptasyllabic verses in the Castilian text.

[4] For a summary of scholarly opinions regarding the size of the medieval Jewish community of Carrión de los Condes, see González and Lagunilla Alonso, *La judería de Carrión*, 24–28.

[5] In addition to San Zoilo, Jews also lived next to the churches of San Julián and San Miguel (Amador de los Ríos, *Historia social, política y religiosa de los judíos*, 1:343). Although the charter granting Jews the right to reside in Carrión de los Condes has been lost, it is mentioned in a document from 1255, and there is reason to speculate that it was issued around the time the Jews of the city of León were granted a similar charter in 1091 (León Tello, *Los judíos de Palencia*, 7).

ABSTRACT In this third chapter I focus on *Proverbios morales* (Moral Proverbs), one of the most important works of medieval Castilian literature. *Proverbios morales* was written around 1350 by Sem Tob de Carrión (ca. 1290–ca. 1369) and dedicated to King Pedro I of Castile and León (r. 1350–1369). Few biographical details on Sem Tob have been uncovered, although it is known that he lived in Carrión de los Condes, a frequently visited stop on the Camino de Santiago. Sem Tob's nearly flawless Castilian *cuaderna vía* versification indicates a period of extensive study with Christian clerics. Sem Tob criticism has yet to focus on the manner by which he learned *cuaderna vía* norms, and I advance the theory that he studied at the Cluniac monastery of San Zoilo, which was the first Castilian Cluniac monastery established on the Camino de Santiago. In *Proverbios morales*, the only Castilian poem Sem Tob produced, he calls for toleration toward Jews and an end to Jewish sectarianism, as such speaking to Christian and Jewish publics. Moreover, Sem Tob's composition of this poem according to *cuaderna vía* norms speaks to his involvement in an interconfessional collaborative culture that supplied him with the tools for voicing his ideas on multiple levels.

Figure 4. Church of the Cross (in Carrión de los Condes),
which was a synagogue in the Middle Ages. (Photo by Gregory B. Kaplan)

This monastery acquired its advocation in the eleventh century after securing the relics of Zoilus (Zoilo), a Cordovan martyr executed at the beginning of the fourth century. The arrival of these relics to the monastery that adopted his name contributed to its growth as a pilgrimage centre for pilgrims travelling on the Camino de Santiago, which was a common phenomenon as I explain elsewhere with respect to the arrival of the relics of Millán to San Millán de la Cogolla.[6] The possession of objects linked to venerated figures enhanced the status of the monasteries where those objects were housed and increased the chances that pilgrims would choose to visit and leave donations. As such, the procurement of relics was a monastic activity that, like the recitation of *cuaderna vía* poetry, was conducted with the aim of producing economic benefits. San Zoilo also acquired assets after officially becoming a Cluniac daughter monastery in 1076, when it began to receive royal donations, including properties in several surrounding villages, .[7]

---

[6] On the history of the relics of San Millán, see Kaplan, *El culto a San Millán*, 81–116.

[7] These properties, which were donated in 1123, were located in the following villages: Villafolfo, Villanueva del Rebollar, Cervatos, Villalumbroso, Santa María de Villaverde, and San Andrés de Congosto (Pérez Celada, *Documentación del monasterio de San Zoilo de Carrión*, 43). See Pérez Celada (ibid., 15–16) on the annexation of San Zoilo to Cluny in 1076.

Figure 5. Interior of the Church of the Cross (in Carrión de los Condes), which was a synagogue in the Middle Ages. (Photo by Gregory B. Kaplan)

In 1220, in gratitude for services rendered to San Zoilo, King Fernando III granted an exemption from an annual royal tax of one hundred *maravedís* to Christian, Jewish, and Muslim residents of the "barrio Sancti Zoili" (San Zoilo neighbourhood).[8] In addition to residing near San Zoilo, Jews also lived in a *judería* (Jewish quarter) located some fifteen minutes' walking distance from that monastery in what is today the parish of San Andrés. The Jews of Carrión formed an economically prosperous community, which was undoubtedly tied to increased pilgrim traffic on the Camino de Santiago, and by 1290 it was paying almost double the taxes paid by other Jewish communities in the region.[9] The close proximity of Jews and Christians created opportunities for contact, evidence of which surfaces in documents such as a decree from 1291 in which a scribe was named to deal with both Jews and Christians living in the region.[10] Another document details a lawsuit from 1479 that concerned properties in Carrión de los Condes owned by monks from San Zoilo. The properties in question were located next to properties owned by a

---

8 Pérez Celada, *Documentación del monasterio de San Zoilo de Carrión*, 142.
9 León Tello, *Los judíos de Palencia*, 105.
10 Pérez Celada, *Documentación del monasterio de San Zoilo de Carrión*, 256–57.

Jew named Baru Pijo, as well as properties owned by a local priest, Pedro García.[11] This historical testimony to coexistence in the vicinity of San Zoilo over the centuries invites speculation as to coexistence within the walls of the monastery.

As a Cluniac daughter monastery, San Zoilo was a place where reading would have been a daily activity, and as a component of a typical Cluniac intellectual culture the composition and recitation of *cuaderna vía* poetry were undoubtedly practised. Evidence of this culture surfaces in a reference to writing instruments and books in the inventory of goods whose ownership was transferred donated to Cluny in 1076 upon enlisting San Zoilo as a daughter monastery.[12] The fact that Jews lived on lands controlled by San Zoilo, and the fact that Christians and Jews lived in close proximity to each other, made it possible for some Jews to have access to the intellectual culture at San Zoilo.

That this access was exploited by individuals such as Sem Tob was a natural outgrowth of Jewish participation in a thriving poetic milieu. Sem Tob's poetic skills were well known to Samuel ben Josef ibn Sasón (d. 1336), a contemporary Jewish poet from the town of Frómista, located some twenty kilometres to the south-east of Carrión de los Condes. As pointed out above, the monastic communities in the two towns were linked, and Ibn Sasón's praise of Sem Tob illustrates that Jewish poets from these towns interacted as well:

> Eminent gentleman in the path of wisdom who weighs and suspends verses, his books are lovely and his sayings are beautiful; he orders his chapters as lines of verse, and with his knowledge overwhelms sages; compared with him the other villagers are like cows. He is as proficient at animal husbandry as he is a poet. He is a composer who breaks rocks and speaks from the Hyssop to the Cedar and his poems are expert and wonderful. The staffs of Rulers are in his hands and he is spread over the Kingdom of Spain.[13]

Ibn Sasón wrote these words in Hebrew, and it stands to reason that his praise is directed toward Sem Tob's Hebrew works, which include a half-dozen liturgical poems that reveal that Sem Tob possessed a knowledge of sacred texts ranging from the Pentateuch to the Talmud. Moreover, the fact that Sem Tob completed a translation of a liturgical work into Arabic from Hebrew speaks to his knowledge of that language, and he also was very familiar with Islamic culture. For example, Sem Tob was certainly familiar with the Arabic rhymed prose (*maqāmā*) tradition, which influenced his composition of *Proverbios morales* as well as his (Hebrew) poem, "Debate between the Pen and the Scissors."[14]

---

11 For a description of the contents of the documents that contain this information, which is housed in Madrid in the Archivo Histórico Nacional, see León Tello, *Los judíos de Palencia*, 139.

12 For a description of the contents of this inventory, see Pérez Celada, *Documentación del monasterio de San Zoilo de Carrión*, 17.

13 Quoted in Klausner, "Reflections on Santob de Carrión," 305 (the translation into English is by Klausner).

14 For descriptions of Seb Tob's Hebrew works, see Díaz-Mas and Mota, "Introduction," 32–34. On the influence of the *maqāmā* on Sem Tob's works, see Wacks, *Double Diaspora in Sephardic Literature*, 111–14, 122–23, and Shepard, *Shem Tov*, 68–69. See Shepard, *Shem Tov*, 79–97, for the English translation (from Hebrew) of "Debate between the Pen and the Scissors."

While Ibn Sasón does not specifically mention Sem Tob's expertise as a *cuaderna vía* poet, the passage above suggests that he may have been aware of Sem Tob's exposure to Christian culture. Ibn Sasón appears to be referring to an association between Sem Tob and the royal court upon declaring that the "staffs of Rulers are in his hands and he is spread over the Kingdom of Spain." Indeed, there is good reason to speculate that the reference to Sem Tob as a carrier of the "staffs of Rulers" alludes to a debt owed to him by Alfonso XI, which is mentioned on two occasions in *Proverbios morales*. Sem Tob first speaks of this debt near the beginning of *Proverbios morales*: "As, for example, the sum promised me, which is of slight worth to you [the king]."[15] Sem Tob concludes the poem with verses in which he again mentions the debt before declaring that he is a Jew: "And the reward that his noble father promised, he will award, as is fitting, to Santob [Sem Tob] the Jew."[16] The debt in question may have involved a loan to the monarchy, as Agustín García Calvo asserts, or perhaps "a moral loan: an award in payment for a service."[17] On another occasion in *Proverbios morales*, Sem Tob's proclamation that he is not the only Jew who has been afforded preferential treatment by the monarchy, "Yet I am not worse than others of my religion who have received good gifts from the King," suggests that he had been compensated previously and that he was on good terms with the king.[18]

Sem Tob dedicated *Proverbios morales* to King Pedro on the eve of a civil war between Pedro and his half-brother, the victorious King Enrique II (r. 1369–1379), which lasted from 1351 until 1369. A penitential (non-*cuaderna vía*) poem that Sem Tob composed in Hebrew around this time may shed light on the evolution of his relationship with the monarchy.[19] The first verses of this poem are informed by refences to rabbinic teachings and to the Old Testament, and announce the traditional Jewish theme of confession, which each Jew is obligated to perform on Yom Kippur (Day of Atonement):

> Lord of the World:
> I contemplate the radiance of youth long gone
> and myself but a shadow of what I was,
> and my sins red as scarlet,
> and my hair white as snow from the years passed in the pursuit of lust.
> I have perverted all the commandments
> and my hopes have ended in frustration.
> I despaired of finding a remedy for my transgressions
> and I ceased seeking repentance.

---

15 Perry, *The "Moral Proverbs" of Santob de Carrión*, 17 (v. 25 [the translation into English is by Perry]); "como la debda mía que a vós muy poco monta" (Carrión, 121 [v. 7a]).

16 Perry, *The "Moral Proverbs" of Santob de Carrión*, 58 (v. 2669 [the translation into English is by Perry]); "E la merçed qu'el noble, su padre, prometió, la terná, como cumple, al Santob el judió" (Carrión, 243 [v. 725a–b]).

17 García Calvo, 162–63. "una deuda moral: un galardón en pago de algún servicio" (*Proverbios morales*, ed. Díaz-Mas and Mota, 28).

18 Perry, *The "Moral Proverbs" of Santob de Carrión*, 19 (v. 161 [the translation into English is by Perry]); "que non só para menos que otros de mi ley / que ovieron muy buenos donadíos del rey" (Carrión, 134 [v. 57a–b]).

19 See Shepard, *Shem Tov*, 102–6, for his English translation of Sem Tob's penitential poem.

> For the day is short and the work is great.
> When shall I make the offering of thanksgiving
> which must be done in the midst of congregation and assembly?
> My sins committed with a will,
> how shall I confess them in the short time remaining
> all the sins committed from the first day of my being?[20]

Sem Tob's declaration that his "youth" is "long gone" is evidence, as Sanford Shepard explains, that this penitential poem "was written in his old age."[21] Sem Tob thus composed the poem during the Castilian civil war, and Shepard identifies Sem Tob's criticism of the struggle between Pedro and Enrique in the following verses:

> Each one follows his own bent.
> They are never satisfied.
> Each attacks the other.
> They are not wise.
> Their hearts are divided and they are both devastated.
> They are never of one mind.
> They never follow one counsel.
> Each of the four follows his own path.
> One desires only to take up the firebrand.
> The other drains the water from the well.
> And they pass by as reed ships.
> One snuffeth up the wind like a crocodile.
> The other digs a pit.
> And they turn their backs to me and do not face me.
> The one deals falsely. The other persecutes.
> One plunders. The other seeks his prey.
> One strikes his fellow with a stone or a fist.
> For they are the children of a generation of perversity.
> A city devastated without a wall!
> While I speak of peace they are at war.
> Their paths are those of wasting and destruction.
> There is no judgment in their goings.
> Their eyes are dimmed and their hearts cannot understand.[22]

In contrast to the good relationship with the monarchy he depicts in *Proverbios morales*, Sem Tob's declaration above that "they turn their backs to me and do not face me" suggests that Sem Tob fell from royal favour during the course of the civil war, perhaps because of his characterization of both Pedro and Enrique as unwise and unwilling to listen to the guidance of those around them.

In *Proverbios morales*, it is the fool who refuses to comprehend reality:

> The fool does not understand, who complains of the sufferings
> that the world often inflicts upon us [all],
> He does not understand that such are the ways of the world:

---

20 Shepard, *Shem Tov*, 102. In his translation, Shepard identifies Sem Tob's references to rabbinic teachings and the Old Testament.
21 Shepard, *Shem Tov*, 98.
22 Shepard, *Shem Tov*, 105–6.

for vile men to be held in esteem,
And for honorable men to be warred against it.
Lift your eyes and consider; you will see that upon the high seas
And upon their banks float [only] dead things,
but in the depths precious stones lie buried.
Likewise, the scale similarly lowers
the fuller plate and raises up the emptier one.
And among the stars of the sky—and He [alone] knows their number—
none suffers eclipse except the sun and the moon.[23]

As Theodore Perry points out, this section of *Proverbios morales* contains several Old Testament allusions that are woven into the narrative as components of Sem Tob's "message to his Jewish readers," namely, "that, eventually, and according to true understanding, the low will be exalted and the oppressed will emerge triumphant."[24] While these verses speak to Sem Tob's Jewish readers, they also speak to his knowledge of contemporary Christian texts. In particular, Sem Tob's use of a Christian source in these verses may reveal his familiarity with *Disciplina clericalis* (Instruction on Life for the Educated), an early twelfth-century collection of moralizing tales of Eastern origin translated from Arabic into Latin by Mosé Sefardí, who adopted the name Petrus Alphonsi (or Pedro Alfonso) after converting from Judaism to Christianity in 1106.

In his edition of *Proverbios morales*, Ignacio González Llubera finds a parallel between stanza 39 ("And among the stars of the sky—and He [alone] knows their number—none suffers eclipse except the sun and the moon") and a section concerning true nobility from part four of *Disciplina clericalis*[25]:

A poet has written some verses on the subject of the adversities of the world which befall those who are of noble birth: he puts them into the mouth of a nobleman, who speaks as follows: "Answer those who despise us for the misfortunes that befall us, and tell them that this world makes life difficult for the man who is noble. Can you not see that the sea brings up mist and spray from its surface, whereas the precious jewels sink to the bottom? And can you not see that there is in the sky a huge number of stars, the exact number of which we do not know, and that not one of them except the sun and moon undergoes an eclipse?" The father answered: "It is due to the unpleasantness of the world that men think that glory is only found in riches."[26]

---

23 Perry, *The "Moral Proverbs" of Santob de Carrión*, 18 v. 89–109 (the translation into English is by Perry). "Non sabe la persona / torpe que se baldona / por las priesas del mundo / qué nos da a menudo; / non sab que la manera / del mundo ésta era: / tener siempre viçiosos / a los ombres astrosos, / e ser d'el guerreados / los omnes onrados. / Alça los ojos, cata: / verás en la mar alta, / e sobre las sus cuestas / andan cosas muertas, / e yacen çafondadas / en él piedras presçiadas; / e el peso así / avaxa otrosí / la más llena balança / e la más vazia alça. / El el çielo estrellas / e sabe cuenta d'ellas / non escuresçen una / sinon el sol e la luna" (Carrión, 127–29 [v. 34a–39d]).

24 Perry, *The "Moral Proverbs" of Santob de Carrión*, 84–85.

25 González Llubera, Introduction to *Proverbios morales*, 4.

26 *The Disciplina clericalis*, 114 (the translation into English is by Quarrie); "Versificator quidam de adversitatibus saeculi, quae super nobiles veniunt, verses fecit istos sub persona nobilium: Dic, inquit, illis qui pro adversitatibus quae nobis accidunt nos contempnunt quod saeculum nulli fecit contrarium nisi nobilibus tantum. Nonne vides quod mare devehit stercora et paleas, et pretiosi lapides in fundum vadunt? Et none vides quod in caelo sunt stellae e quibus nes cimus numerum?

The source for Sem Tob's knowledge of *Disciplina clericalis* merits reconsideration, in particular because it is a work to which he alludes on several occasions in *Proverbios morales*.[27] One occasion occurs in a verse in which Sem Tob elaborates on covetousness and envy: "It is from acquiring a thing that there arises a desire for another, bigger and better. For want comes from excess."[28] This verse recalls a passage from chapter 21 of *Disciplina clericalis*: "He who desires much, is always ill in his hunger for more."[29] In a stanza concerning covetousness and true wealth that appears further on in *Proverbios morales*, "The whole day long he is exhausted, hounded to get it, and through the night he is anxious out of fear of losing it,"[30] Sem Tob borrows from chapter 21 of *Disciplina clericalis*, in which Alphonsi writes: "Yet another said: 'The man who hoards money works much, and worries himself into insomnia for fear of losing it. But at the last he has the sorrow of losing what he has gained.'"[31]

The fact that Sem Tob knew *Disciplina clericalis* is not surprising in itself insofar as the work was popular during the late Middle Ages. There are more than sixty extant manuscripts of *Disciplina clericalis* that date from the twelfth through the fourteenth centuries, and it was translated into French during the early thirteenth century. In the fifteenth century, the Latin text was translated into several European languages and disseminated in printed editions.[32] The first translation into Hebrew of part of *Disciplina clericalis* was produced during the sixteenth century.[33] While it is possible that Sem Tob consulted an early version of the translated Hebrew text that would be published two centuries later, in light of the popularity of *Disciplina clericalis* during Sem Tob's lifetime it is more likely that he was familiar with the Latin text. *Disciplina clericalis* was used in

---

At insuper nulla quidem patitur eclipsim praeter solem et lunam. Et pater: Ex temporis inertia accidit quia homines in divitiis solum iudicant gloriandum" (Alfonso, *Disciplina clericalis*, ed. González Palencia, 18). Perry identifies Alphonsi's source ("A poet has written") as the eleventh century Islamic poet from Seville, al Mu'tamid (Perry, *The "Moral Proverbs" of Santob de Carrión*, 79–80).

27 For a list of the verses from *Proverbios morales* that recall passages in *Disciplina clericalis*, see Díaz-Mas and Mota, "Introduction," 85.

28 Perry, *The "Moral Proverbs" of Santob de Carrión*, 29 (v. 797) (the translation into English is by Perry); "De alcançar una cosa naçe cobdiçia de otra / mayor e más lazrosa, que mengua vien de sobra" (Carrión, 144 [v. 216a–b]).

29 *The Disciplina clericalis*, 141 (the translation into English is by Quarrie); "Qui multa cupit, semper maiorum fame tabescit" (Alfonso, *Disciplina clericalis*, ed. González Palencia, 57).

30 Perry, *The "Moral Proverbs" of Santob de Carrión*, 30 v. 865 (the translation into English is by Perry); "todo el día lazrado, corrido por traerlo, / e la noche cuitado por miedo de perderlo" (Carrión, 164 [v. 233a–b]).

31 *The Disciplina clericalis*, 141 (the translation into English is by Quarrie). The Latin text is as follows: "Alius: Qui pecuniam congregat, multum laborat et vigiliis tabescit ne perdat; ad ultimum dolet quiniam perdit quod obtinuerat" (Alfonso, *Disciplina clericalis*, ed. González Palencia, 58). On the *Disciplina clericalis* as a source for this verse, see Stein, *Untersuchungen über die Proverbios Morales*, 67.

32 For a list of the *Disciplina clericalis* from the twelfth through the fifteenth centuries, see Tolan, *Petrus Alfonsi and his Medieval Readers*, 199–204, and for a review of these early printed editions of *Disciplina clericalis*, see *The Disciplina clericalis*, 197–98.

33 On this Hebrew edition, see Tolan, *Petrus Alfonsi and his Medieval Readers*, 248n1.

the thirteenth century as a "handbook" for preachers who found it to be "a gold mine of exempla" for their sermons.[34] It is thus possible to envision a link between Sem Tob's knowledge of *Disciplina clericalis* and his contact with Christian clerics, from whom Sem Tob may have learned the Latin necessary to access the text. The location where this interaction would have occurred would have been the monastery of San Zoilo, the only place in the vicinity with a library that might have held a copy of *Disciplina clericalis* (or perhaps a copy of a fragment of the text). It would be logical to speculate that Sem Tob's knowledge of *Disciplina clericalis* was acquired contemporaneous to the time he acquired a knowledge of the *cuaderna vía* norms he would employ during the composition of *Proverbios morales*.

Proverbios morales reveals Sem Tob's mastery of Castilian syllabic computation. This is evident in the many verses in *Proverbios morales* in which no contact occurs between word-final and word-initial vowels. One example is the second verse of the initial stanza, in which Sem Tob announces his provenance: "que viene dezir Santo, judío de Carrión."[35] Although Sem Tob separates his verses into couplets rather quatrains, his consonant rhyme follows the *cuaderna vía* tradition and reveals his command of Castilian phonetics. These are all indications that he studied *cuaderna vía* poetry and, in light of the privileged condition of the Jews of Carrión de los Condes, there are solid grounds for speculating that his "Christian" education occurred at the San Zoilo monastic school.

Sem Tob's profound knowledge of Castilian syllabic division is also displayed in the many verses in *Proverbios morales* in which contact does occur between word-final and word-initial vowels. In order to achieve a fourteen-syllable count in such verses, hiatus is at times necessary. Sem Tob uses hiatus in *Proverbios morales* with an efficiency that distinguishes this work from those by early Jewish *cuaderna vía* poets such as the anonymous authors of "El Dio alto que los çielos sostiene," "Cuando el rey Nimrod al campo saldriya," and "Cuando a Yerušaláyim vide en tanta fatiga," who employ verses of differing lengths. Although the verses in these anonymous poems in which there is no contact between word-final and word-initial vowels reveals that the poets did attempt to achieve a dodecasyllabic regularity, their use of hiatus (and synalepha) in verses in which such contact does occur is impossible to determine with certainty.

Sem Tob, however, like early Christian *cuaderna vía* poets, possessed the ability to use hiatus consistently, which is revealed in the regular fourteen-syllable count of his verses. Such hiatus is the norm in Berceo's *Milagros*, for example, in verses such as "palavra es oscura" ("is an obscure parable"), in which the hiatus between word final -a ("palavra") and word-initial -e ("es") creates one half, or one seven-syllable hemistich, of a fourteenth-syllable alexandrine ("palavra es oscura, esponerla queremos").[36] Sem Tob frequently incorporates the same type of hiatus into verses such as "monta el tu pecado" ("to that same degree does your sin compare") in which the word-final -a

---

34 Tolan, *Petrus Alfonsi and his Medieval Readers*, 139.

35 Carrión, 119 (v. 1a); "[this discourse] which Santob, the Jew from Carrión, comes forward to speak" (Perry, *The "Moral Proverbs" of Santob de Carrión*, 17 v. 1; the translation into English is by Perry).

36 Berceo, *Milagros*, 72 (v. 16b); "is an obscure parable and we wish to explain it" (Berceo, *Miracles*, 23 [v. 16b; the translation into English is by Mount and Cash]).

("monta") is separated through hiatus from word-initial -e ("el") to form two syllables, as such resulting in a heptasyllabic hemistich that complements the following one to form a fourteen-syllable alexandrine: "monta el tu pecado a su misericordia."[37] At the same time, in keeping with fourteenth-century norms, synalepha is evident throughout *Proverbios morales*, including in hemistiches in which contact occurs between the same vowels, such as "Entendí que en callar," which must incorporate synalepha in order for it to be heptasyllabic.[38] In *Milagros*, Berceo employs hiatus to separate such vowels, as in: "que en piedes andamos."[39]

On other occasions, Sem Tob vacillates between hiatus and synalepha, as in the following initial hemistiches from sequential verses in *Proverbios morales*: "e astroso garrote" ("And a miserable catapult") and "e algunt roto pellote" ("and a torn skin"). In the case of the first hemistich, hiatus is employed between "e" and "astroso" in order to produce seven syllables within a fourteen-syllable alexandrine: "e astroso garrote faze muy çiertos trechos."[40] In the hemistich that begins the next verse, "e algunt roto pellote," synalepha is needed between "e" and "algunt" in order to produce the first seven syllables of the fourteen-syllable verse, "e algunt roto pellote encubre blancos pechos," although hiatus occurs between word-final -e ("pellote") and word-initial e- ("encubre") to mark the division between hemistiches.[41] The two hemistiches in question from Sem Tob, "e astroso garrote" and "e algunt roto pellote," reveal a unique feature of his alexandrine, which incorporates internal consonant rhyme between hemistiches (-ote) in sequential verses.[42] While there are some exceptions, this internal consonant rhyme is employed by Sem Tob throughout *Proverbios morales*, and speaks to his ability to not only imitate the *cuaderna vía* poetic form, but to participate in its evolution as well by exploiting the acoustic potential of the *medial caesura* within the alexandrine verse.

David Wacks has underscored the role of Christian *cuaderna vía* clerical poets as "intellectual intermediaries" who poeticized "learned knowledge" for their listening publics.[43] As a work whose creation speaks to a peaceful coexistence between Christian clerical teachers and Jewish students, *Proverbios morales* reveals Sem Tob's learned appreciation for *cuaderna vía* poetry as a form of indoctrination through public recita-

---

[37] Carrión, 126 (v. 27b); "to that same degree does your sin compare to His mercy" (Perry, *The "Moral Proverbs" of Santob de Carrión*, 18 [v. 69]; the translation into English is by Perry).

[38] Carrión, 134 (v. 56a); "I concluded that silence" (Perry, *The "Moral Proverbs" of Santob de Carrión*, 19 [v. 157]; the translation into English is by Perry).

[39] Berceo, *Milagros*, 72 (v. 17a); "and stand upright" (Berceo, *Miracles*, 23 [v. 17a]; the translation into English is by Mount and Cash).

[40] Carrión, 135 (v. 61a); "And a miserable catapult can be most accurate" (Perry, *The "Moral Proverbs" of Santob de Carrión*, 20 [v. 177]; the translation into English is by Perry).

[41] Carrión, 135 (v. 61b); "and a torn skin can cover up white breasts" (Perry, *The "Moral Proverbs" of Santob de Carrión*, 20 [v. 177]; the translation into English is by Perry).

[42] For example, "Confessóse el monge e fizo penitencia" (Berceo, *Milagros*, 88 [v. 99a]); "The monk confessed and did penance" (Berceo, *Miracles*, 35 [v. 99a]; the translation into English is by Mount and Cash).

[43] Wacks, *Double Diaspora in Sephardic Literature*, 108.

tion. Christian *cuaderna vía* poems could be used as tools for guiding Christian pilgrims toward reverence for a religious hierarchy, which was symbolized by the depiction of the Virgin or a saint as a mediator between Salvation and earthly perils. In this context, Berceo's *Milagros* provides the most well-known example of the capacity for *cuaderna vía* poetry to popularize Marian devotion, one of the most powerful forms of medieval spirituality. Berceo's work serves as a blueprint for explaining to pilgrims the many ways by which the Virgin could lead them away from sin in their daily lives and help them find the path toward Salvation, and Sem Tob undoubtedly recognized that he could exploit the *cuaderna vía* poetic form in order to create a platform for guiding his public toward greater social harmony.

Sem Tob composed *Proverbios morales* "for the benefit of all," that is, in order to reach both Christians and Jews.[44] The Castilian civil war that pitted supporters of King Pedro against his half-bother Enrique exacerbated previous tensions that stemmed from economic crises in which Jewish tax collectors were cast into the role of scapegoat, and Pedro's support for his Jewish subjects played a pivotal role in turning public opinion against him and contributed to outbreaks of popular violence directed at Jewish communities. It is with the hope of avoiding such an outcome that Sem Tob appeals to King Pedro in *Proverbios morales* for impartial justice in the face of growing anti-Semitism:

> There is no man so cowardly as he who has done evil, nor hero so great as he who is in the right.
>
> There is nothing so shameless as a just judge, who is indifferent to both harm and profit.
>
> With utter lack of mercy he condemns to death both poor and rich; he considers the great and the lowly with an equal eye.
>
> He flatters the lord no more than his servant; he does not favor a king over his functionaries.
>
> But the evil judge is much too generous with justice: he awards it to him who is without justice, thus turning a bow into a straight stick.
>
> In truth, the world subsists through three things: justice, truth, and peace, which comes from these.
>
> Justice is the cornerstone; of all three, is has the greatest worth.
>
> For justice uncovers truth, and with truth comes peace and friendship.[45]

---

44 Perry, *The "Moral Proverbs" of Santob de Carrión*, 17 (v. 5; the translation into English is by Perry); "comunalment trobado" (Carrión, 119 [v. 2a]).

45 Perry, *The "Moral Proverbs" of Santob de Carrión*, 38 (v. 1349–77; the translation into English is by Perry); "nin omre tan cobarde com el que mal ha fecho, / ni barragán tan grande com el que tien derecho; / nin ha tan sin vergüença cosa com el derecho: / del daño esa fuerça faze que del provecho. / Tan sin piadat mata al pobre com al rico / e con un ojo cata al grande e al chico: / al señor non lisonja más que al serbiçial, / al rey non avantaja sobre su ofiçial; / pero el jüez malo, él fázese muy franco: / al que non lo tien, dalo; faze vara del arco. / El mundo la verdat de tres cosas mantién: / juïzio e verdat e paz que d'ellos vien. / E el juïzio es la piedra çimental; / de todas estas tres él es la que más val, / ca el juïzio faz escobrir la verdat, / e con la verdat faz venir a amizdat" (Carrión, 183–84 [v. 354a–361b]).

In declaring that a brazenly "just judge [...] does not favor a king over his functionaries," Sem Tob advocates for protecting the tenuous position of Jewish collectors of royal taxes, whose communities were attacked during times of economic crisis. Sem Tob's call for "peace and friendship" is a plea for social harmony, which was also necessary after 1348, when outbreaks of the Black Plague in Spain (and throughout Europe) intensified popular anti-Jewish sentiment. While Sem Tob was motivated to compose *Proverbios morales* because he and his fellow Jews faced great danger as anti-Semtism escalated parallel to political tensions, Sem Tob was also concerned about tensions within the Jewish community.

Sem Tob was undoubtedly well versed in an age-old tradition according to which rabbinic revelations of the Oral Law were afforded primacy while those who questioned rabbinic doctrines never enjoyed the favour of authority and were at times subject to persecution by Rabbinites. The fact that Sem Tob's Hebrew penitential poem was adopted into the liturgy as a prayer during Yom Kippur speaks directly to his standing as a rabbinic authority, and as such implicitly representing one side of a polemic between Rabbinites and anti-Rabbinites, or Karaites. During the fourteenth century, the majority of Jews in Carrión are thought to have been Karaites, and Sem Tob was undoubtedly in a unique position as a bridge between Jewish sects.[46] While Sem Tob might have chosen to disseminate exclusively pro-rabbinic ideas, much in line with the Christian *cuaderna vía* tendency to impart religious doctrines, in *Proverbios morales* this is not the case. Sem Tob chooses to play the role of mediator by voicing the opposition to Rabbinism in response to his contemporary social circumstances and in order to convey the urgency among Jews to set aside internal disputes in the face of mounting majority resentments.

Sem Tob composed his only poem in Castilian at a time when deteriorating circumstances called for him to publicly voice the potential danger of historical divisions within Spanish Judaism. The fact that Sem Tob did not produce such a poem until late in his life may signify that he did not achieve a mastery of Castilian *cuaderna vía* norms until that time. In light of this possibility, it is interesting to speculate that Sem Tob studied *cuaderna vía* poetry with the specific intention of exploiting the propagandistic potential of this form of public expression. As a work that conveys the urgency among Jews to set aside internal conflicts in the face of mounting anti-Judaism, *Proverbios morales* serves as an important platform for recalling lessons to be learned from recent and ancient Jewish history.

The escalation of tensions between Rabbinites and Karaites in medieval Spain was an iteration of a Jewish sectarianism that traced its roots to the emergence of religious authority after the destruction in 70 CE of the Second Temple. The loss of this spiritual centre created a vacuum that was filled by Pharisees, adherents to rabbinic interpretations that were thought to repeat doctrines (the Oral Law) given to Moses along with the Pentateuch. Opposition to Pharisees evolved among sects collectively known as Saddu-

---

[46] León Tello (*Los judíos de Palencia*, 8) affirms that Karaites constituted the majority of the Jews in Carrión, and that this community of Karaites must have been the only one permitted to remain in place after a royal decree by Alfonso VI expelled Karaites from Castile as discussed below.

cees, that is, followers of a strictly literal interpretation of the Pentateuch. The threat to Pharisees posed by Sadducees is explained in observations made by the Romano-Jewish historian Flavius Josephus (b. 37–d. ca. 100) in *The Jewish War*: "The Sadducees, the second order, deny Fate altogether and hold that God is incapable of either committing sin or seeing it; they say that men are free to choose between good and evil, and each individual must decide which he will follow."[47] According to Josephus in *The Antiquities of the Jews*, by lending primacy to individual freedom of choice Sadducees legitimized their rejection of Pharisees on the grounds that rabbinic traditions lacked documentation: "the Pharisees have delivered to the people a great many observances by succession from their fathers, which are not written in the laws of Moses; and for that reason it is that the Sadducees reject them, and say that we are to esteem those observances to be obligatory which are in the written word, but are not to observe what are derived from the tradition of our forefathers."[48]

After the destruction of the Second Temple, anti-Rabbinism resurfaced among Jews in Babylonian exile as Jewish spiritual authority was transferred from a centralized polity governed by Mosaic Law to centres where generation after generation of rabbis revealed the Oral Law, which Rabbinites believed to possess the same authority as the Law given to Moses. The rejection of rabbinic interpretations of the Old Testament, including those codified in the Talmud, was influenced during the early Middle Ages by contact with Islam. In the cosmopolitan centres of Constantinople and Damascus, anti-Rabbinism was nurtured by Islamic concepts such as lending primacy to sacred writings in determining spiritual law and independent investigation of ambiguous passages in sacred texts.

The transmission of anti-Rabbinism was to all corners of the Mediterranean was facilitated by Islamic military conquests during the seventh and eighth centuries. As a result of the tolerant nature of Islamic hegemony in southern Spain, ideas arriving from the East informed cross-cultural dialogues in literary, scientific, and religious spheres. The continuation of this hegemony for several centuries produced the political stability that fueled economic prosperity and a flourishing culture in which exposure to Middle Eastern schools of thought encouraged Jewish defiance of traditional religious authority.

The medieval conflict between Rabbinites and anti-Rabbinites was exacerbated around the figure of Anan ben David (b. ca. 715–d. ca. 795), who gained a following among Babylonian anti-Rabbinites from various groups, a movement that became Karaism, the expansion of which essentially renewed the process that had led to the formation of the Sadducees in ancient times.[49] The opposition to rabbinic authority around which Karaism formed is evident in the earliest known account of Anan's activities by Natronay bar Hilay (b. ca. 795–d.ca. 865), the ninth-century *Gaon*, or chief sage, of the

---

47 Josephus, *The Jewish War*, 130. The ancient origins of the Sadducees are indicated by Josephus in *The Antiquities of the Jews*: "The Jews had for a great while had three sects of philosophy peculiar to themselves; the sect of the Essens, and the sect of the Sadducees, and the third sort of opinions was that of those called Pharisees" (bk. 18, chap. 1, para. 2).
48 Josephus, *The Antiquities of the Jews*, book 13, chap. 10, para. 6.
49 On the influence of Islamic ideologies on Karaism, see Kohler, "Karaites and Karaism," 438–39.

Babylonian Jewish academy in Sura. The account is found in *Seder Rav 'Amram Gaon bar Sheshna* (Prayerbook of Rabbi Amram, the Chief Sage of Sura), which was the first Jewish prayer book and in which Natronay accuses Karaites of being anti-Rabbinic heretics.[50] The attention paid by Natronay to denouncing Karaism reveals that the movement had concretized while acquiring more followers.

As its growth was fueled by contact with Muslim scholars and theologians working to develop doctrines that questioned monolithic orthodoxy, Karaites "unite[d] under its aegis the chief opposition to the central controls administered by exilarchs and academies in the name of the Talmud."[51] At the zenith of the Cordovan Caliphate, one of the most renowned intellectuals, the Muslim historian and theologian Ibn Hazm (b. 994–d. 1064), detected the fruits of this dialogue in Spain. According to Ibn Hazm, Karaism had acquired a following among Jews in the cities of Toledo and Talavera, which reveals that it had gained a foothold in Castile.[52]

Karaite preachers and scholars, including Cid Abu'l-Taras in Castile and Benjamin Nahawandi in Persia, worked during the eleventh and twelfth centuries to popularize resistance to Rabbinic Judaism around the time Ibn Hazm made his observations, and this practice was soon met by opposition. Rather than engage in an intracommunal dialogue regarding Karaite doctrines, including ideas espoused by Nahawandi that actually brought Karaism closer to the Talmud, swift retribution from Christian authorities was sought.[53] Against a heresy that could not be extinguished, anti-Karaite persecution organized by the Spanish rabbinate and influential Jews at court was successful in securing royal decrees in 1178 and 1232 that prohibited Karaism.[54]

The perceived magnitude of the Karaite threat informs *The Book of Tradition* (1160–1161) by the Cordovan historian and philosopher Abraham ibn Daud (b. ca. 1110–d. ca. 1180). *The Book of Tradition* is the most important medieval work against Jewish sectarianism and an ardent defence of an uninterrupted rabbinic tradition since biblical times. Claims by Ibn Daud that Karaites "never did anything of benefit for Israel, nor produced a book demonstrating the cogency of the Torah or work of general knowledge or even a single poem, hymn or verse of consolation"[55] exemplify his attempt at diminishing the importance of Karaism.

Ibn Daud sacrifices historical accuracy to achieve his main goal of establishing the continuity of Rabbinic Judaism, and it may be said that he is motivated more by a desire to put a quick end to what he perceived as a long-standing threat than an attempt to engage in a polemic concerning particular Karaite doctrines. The popularity of Karaism is greatly downplayed by Ibn Daud, who claims that the quasi epic figure of Rabbi Joseph

---

50 Martin Cohen, "Anan ben David," 135.
51 Baron, *A Social and Religious History of the Jews*, 9:230.
52 The translation into English of Ibn Hazm is by Gerson Cohen (Daud, *The Book of Tradition*, xlvi).
53 On the approximation of Nahawandi's ideas to Talmudic law, see Kohler, "Karaites and Karaism," 438–39.
54 On this period in anti-Karaite persecution, see Sáinz de la Maza, "Alfonso de Valladolid y los caraítas."
55 Daud, *The Book of Tradition*, 99–100.

ha Nasi Ibn Ferruziel (d. ca. 1145), a royal physician, all but eliminated the presence of Karaism in Castile by convincing King Alfonso VI to expel Karaites from Castilian towns. In order to further downplay the popularity of Karaism, Ibn Daud provides an anachronistic account of the birth of the Karaite movement in Spain, in which he ridicules its heretical origins:

> When the Jews used to celebrate the festival of Tabernacles on the Mount of Olives, they would encamp on the mountain in groups and greet each other warmly. The heretics would encamp before them like two little flocks of goats. Then the rabbis would take out a scroll of the Torah and pronounce a ban on the heretics right to their faces, while the latter remained silent like dumb dogs.
>
> Among those [heretics] living in the Holy Land there was *al-Sheikh* Abu'l-Faraj, may his bones be committed to hell. It happened that a certain fool from Castile, named Cid Abu'l-Taras, went over there and met the wicked *al-Sheikh* Abu'l-Faraj, who seduced him into heresy. Under the guidance of the latter, Abu'l-Taras composed a work animated by seduction and perversion, which he introduced into Castile and [by means of which] he led many astray. When Abu'l-Taras passed on to hell, he was survived by his accursed wife, whom [his adherents] used to address as *al-Mu allima* and on whom they relied for authoritative tradition. They would ask each other what *Mu allima*'s usage was, and they would follow suit. [This went on] until the rise to power of the Nasi R. Joseph b. Ferruziel, surnamed Cidellus, who suppressed them even beyond their former lowly state. He drove them out of all the strongholds of Castile except for one, which he granted them, since he did not want to put them to death (inasmuch as capital punishment is not administered at the present time). However, after his death, the heretics erupted until the reign of King Don Alfonso son of Raimund, king of kings, the *Emperador*. In his reign there rose *nesiim* who pursued the ways of their fathers and suppressed the heretics [again].⁵⁶

In spite of efforts to suppress Karaism in Castile, its spread caused the rabbinate to seek royal support for the expulsion of Karaites from public places, which was decreed in 1109. However, the repetition of this decree in 1148 reflected the continued popularity of Karaism. By 1178, Karaism had become so widespread in Carrión de los Condes that courtier rabbis sought assistance from the king, which resulted in a royal decree that compelled Karaites to adopt rabbinic norms.⁵⁷

Ibn Daud's disparaging attitude toward Karaism is amplified and used as a tool for fomenting tensions among Jews in *Mostrador de justicia* (Revealer of Justice), which was written by a theologian from Burgos named Abner (b. ca. 1270–d. ca. 1347). Abner was a contemporary of Sem Tob who converted from Judaism to Christianity and became a renowned anti-Jewish polemicist. *Mostrador* was originally written by Abner in Hebrew before it was translated into Castilian in the fourteenth century. In this work, Abner reveals early on that one of his principal motives for composing *Mostrador* is to expose the conflict between Rabbinites and anti-Rabbinites: "most of the Jews believe in the teachings of their Talmudic sages, and only very few dare to go against those sages.

---

56 Daud, *The Book of Tradition*, 94–95.
57 On these royal decrees, see León Tello, *Los judíos de Palencia*, 8–9.

Therefore, their disrepute becomes greater when we find evidence against them based on their great sages who they revere and honour."[58]

Abner inherits from Ibn Daud (whose *Book of Tradition* is cited on a number of occasions in *Mostrador*) the tendency toward anachronistic accounts of historical anti-Rabbinism. Abner thus depicts Sadducees as a continuation of a biblical tradition and Sadducees, rather than Karaites, inhabit the Castilian towns of Carrión de los Condes and Burgos. Abner groups all anti-Rabbinites as heretics and points out that the expression of this sizeable group ("muchos omnes que niegan el ssu Talmud dellos" ["many men who deny their Talmud"]) is suppressed:

> It is said that the Jewish heretic, the one who rejects what the Jews have received from their ancestors [...] cannot be straightened out for any reason shared by other Jews, who disdain and cast doubt on the view of those who deny what has been understood, even those things that could straighten them out and resolve their doubts. This explains why there are found among the Jews many men who deny the Talmud.[59]

Abner's desire to exploit tensions between Rabbinites and anti-Rabbinites is evident on other occasions in *Mostrador* as scholars have concluded. Salo Baron suggests an influence of Karaism on the last chapter of Abner's text: "This chapter, devoted to a detailed critique of the Maimonidean Code, bears many similarities with the attacks on Rabbinite law by Karaites."[60] Ryan Szpiech depicts Abner's attitude in terms that recall anti-Rabbinism since the time of the Sadducees:

> Rather than attacking the Rabbinical writing or his Jewish reader directly, however, he instead faults the early rabbis who, he claims, knew that Jesus was the expected Messiah but refused to teach others what they discerned in Scriptures and traditional authorities. They did this not out of ignorance but out of their ill will against Jesus. This deliberate concealment by the original sages was then perpetuated by later Jewish leaders and handed down as tradition within the Jewish community, and it is up to the righteous individual Jew to break this transmission and fix his own tradition.[61]

Abner's reverence for Karaism fuels a dialogue between *Mostrador* and *Proverbios morales* that speaks to an adversarial relationship between Abner and Sem Tob described by Shepard: "[t]he persistence of Karaite tendencies had a notable effect on Abner of Burgos [...] whose polemic against Judaism [*Mostrador de justicia*] exerted a

---

[58] "los más de los judios creen en los dichos de ssus ssabios del Talmud, e muy pocos sson dellos que ossan yr contra aquellos sabios. Por ende enfforçarsse-a la nuestra rrazon contra ellos quando nos aduremos prueuas contra ellos de los sus grandes ssabios abtenticos e onrrados entrellos" (Abner, *Mostrador de justicia*, ed. Mettman, 1:43).

[59] "Como que diz que el ereje judio, el que despreçia en lo que tienen rresçebido los judios de ssus anteçessores [...] tal omne como éste non puede auer endereçamiento por ninguna rrazon quel rrazonassen los otros judios, despues que desdennan e ponen dubda en sus opiniones rresçebidas dellos e que niega[n] las opiniones entendidas, las que podrian endereçar e ssoltar ssus dubhas. E por esto sson fallados en los judios muchos omnes que niegan el ssu Talmud dellos" (Abner, *Mostrador de justicia*, ed. Mettman, 2:419).

[60] Baron, *A Social and Religious History of the Jews*, 9:305n32.

[61] Szpiech, *Conversion and Narrative*, 153.

profound influence on Shem Tov's literary works."[62] Similarly, Perry posits that Sem Tob responded to "the danger of the Jewish informer to the gentile authorities, such as Abner of Burgos" when he depicted the rise to power of the vile man in *Proverbios morales*[63]:

> The vile man acts in the opposite way: lowering himself to those greater than he, he acts high and mighty with his inferiors.
>
> He portrays his bad fortune as more than twice as bad as it really is, and in good fortune he astounds everyone.
>
> When his luck is bad, he is lower than the earth; but in good times he challenges heaven itself.
>
> He who would like to hear the reputation of the vile man so as to recognize him openly when he sees him:
>
> He does nothing on request but submits to force; break him and he will immediately obey you.
>
> I consider him as a bow in all his activities; for until he is bent he can do no good.[64]

Although it is not known whether Abner and Sem Tob met in person, the theories of Shepard and Perry regarding the influence of the former on the latter are borne out by a comparative analysis of Sem Tob's "vyllano," or "vile man," who is presented in contrast to the "omre noble," or "noble man." Sem Tob writes that "The noble man is accustomed to raise himself up to the great of this world and to show himself humble and docile with the lowly. / He shows his greatness to strangers and shows great humility to those that have fallen low."[65] However, the vile man "astounds everyone" and "challenges heaven itself." Whereas Sem Tob guides the reader toward the behaviour of the noble man, he also draws attention to the success of the vile man, whose actions are not examples to follow because they contribute to social discord (requiring the use of "force"), which is, in turn, a component of Sem Tob's broader message to King Pedro. By extension, it may be argued that Sem Tob endeavours to recall sectarian oppression in order to warn against its being directed toward Jews. In other words, Sem Tob is reminding Jews of the danger of allowing sectarian divisions to legitimize anti-Jewish persecution in Christian eyes.

---

62 Shepard, *Shem Tov*, 16. With regard to what I term "reverence" for Karaite anti-Rabbinism, Shepard writes: "Abner revived the slumbering rationalism of the Karaites that had been utilized before to call into question the authority of the *Talmud*" (*Shem Tov*, 29).

63 Perry, *The "Moral Proverbs" of Santob de Carrión*, 129n32.

64 The translation into English is by Perry, *The "Moral Proverbs" of Santob de Carrión*, 34 (v. 1081–101); "Su revés del villano: baxas a los mayores, / e alto e loçano se faz a los menores; / más de cuanto es, dos tanta, muestra su malandança, / e al mundo espanta en la su buenandança; / en la su malandança es más baxo que tierra, / en la su buenandança al çielo quier dar guerra. / El que oír quisiere las mañas del villano / porque cuando lo viere lo conoçca de mano: / non faz cosa por ruego, e la premia consiente; / castígalo, e luego te será obediente. / Com el arco le cuento yo en todo su fecho: / fasta quel fazen tuerto él nunca faz derecho" (Carrión, 172–73 [v. 287a–92b]).

65 The translation into English is by Perry, *The "Moral Proverbs" of Santob de Carrión*, 33 (v. 1065–69); "Usa el omre noble a los altos alçarse; / simple e convenible a los vaxos mostrarse; / muestra la su grandeza a los desconoçidos / e la su gran simpleza a los baxos caídos" (Carrión, 171–72 [v. 283a–84b]).

Sem Tob's depiction above of the vile man begins by symbolically recalling the social circumstances described by Abner: "The vile man acts in the opposite way: lowering himself to those greater than he, he acts high and mighty with his inferiors." By declaring that vileness is achieved by "act[ing] in the opposite way [and] lowering himself to those greater than he," Sem Tob recognizes the process by which the flames of Christian anti-Judaism were ignited through Abner's depiction of sectarian persecution. Abner's aforementioned declaration that only few dare to challenge the rabbinate evokes the fact that these challenges were met with harsh retribution, which stirred anti-Jewish sentiment, a situation that Sem Tob also recalls for his Jewish and royal publics as a means of demonstrating "the potential harm from such an individual to the entire community."[66] Abner's efforts were ultimately successful, and in 1336 he "obtained a decree from Alfonso XI requiring the examination of Hebrew books for alleged blasphemy against Jesus and the Holy Family."[67]

Perry explains that similar harm could result from "the crucial moment of [...] the transfer of royal power" to a king who might issue anti-Jewish decrees, although such harm could also be produced through acts committed by Jews against Jews.[68] A figure evoked by the "vile man" of Sem Tob for "lowering himself to those greater than he" was the previously mentioned Rabbi Ibn Ferruziel, who conducted his attack on Karaites in 1109 by personally subjecting them to "all types of humiliation."[69] This mortification of Karaites was essentially repeated when, after Karaites had regrouped, Rabbi Yehuda ben Ezra, the royal steward to Alfonso VII of Castile and León (r. 1126–1157), "asked the king not to permit the heretics to speak throughout Castile."[70] In the wake of the success of Karaism in Carrión de los Condes, it was the royal physician, Josef Alfácar, who obtained the decree from Alfonso VIII (r. 1158–1214) that forced Rabbinism on Karaites.

While they are known historically as "noble men"—for example, the quasi epic figure of Ibn Ferruziel earned the epithet Cidellus, or "little Cid," and helped many Jews escape to northern Spain from increasingly intolerant Islamic rule in the south—the involvement of Ibn Ferruziel, Ben Ezra, and Alfácar in obtaining royal sanction of the oppression of Karaites is, according to Sem Tob's reasoning, "the opposite way" of the noble behaviour that he describes ("The noble man is accustomed to raise himself up to the great of this world and to show himself humble and docile with the lowly. / He shows his greatness to strangers and shows great humility to those that have fallen low"). The lack of humility displayed by Ibn Ferruziel, Ben Ezra, and Alfácar is condemned by Sem Tob, as it is by Abner, albeit for different motives. Abner endeavours to underscore the

---

66 Perry, *The "Moral Proverbs" of Santob de Carrión*, 129.
67 Shepard, *Shem Tov*, 28.
68 Perry, *The "Moral Proverbs" of Santob de Carrión*, 129.
69 "toda clase de humillaciones" (quoted in Sáinz de la Maza, "Alfonso de Valladolid y los caraítas," 19).
70 "pidió al rey que no dejara abrir la boca a los herejes en toda la tierra de Castilla" (quoted in Sáinz de la Maza, "Alfonso de Valladolid y los caraítas," 19–20).

fact that Jewish sectarianism was met with rabbinic oppression in order to provide an insider's perspective as ideological fuel for enhancing an extant anti-Jewish animus.

For Sem Tob, the veiled reference to questionable acts performed by respected rabbis is a condemnation of the use of intimidation to quell sectarian sentiment, as such amplifying his call to King Pedro for tolerant policies. The urgency of this call responded to the fear that Pedro would inherit the posture of his father, Alfonso XI, who "fluctuated between favor and persecution."[71] In light of increasing popular anti-Judaism tied to a variety of factors, including outbreaks of the Black Plague and economic crises, the words of both Abner and Sem Tob ultimately proved prescient. Abner influenced other apostates such as Rabbi Solomon ha Levi of Burgos (b. ca. 1351–d. 1435), who became Pablo de Santa María upon converting to Christianity. Santa María's conversion was one of thousands that occurred in 1391 after a wave of anti-Jewish violence swept through Spain. This violence marked the culmination of an increase during the late 1300s in popular anti-Semitism, which was fuelled by outbreaks of the Black Plague and economic crises that cast Jews into the role of scapegoat.[72] While conversion enabled Jews to escape popular violence, it did not equate to assimilation within the broader Christian community for reasons that lie beyond the scope of the present study.[73] The first generation of *conversos* produced in 1391, or New Christians, would never cease being perceived by Old Christians as religiously inferior, a stigma that would be passed on to future generations of *conversos*, whose Jewish ancestry would intensify the inquisitorial scrutiny cast upon them. In spite of the fact that *conversos* were perceived as inferior Christians, conversions continued to occur until the remaining Jews who refused to convert were expelled from Spain in 1492.

Testimony of the importance of the legacy of Sem Tob is revealed in a Castilian prologue to *Proverbios morales* composed several decades before the expulsion: "For, without doubt, these verses are notable writings which every person should learn by heart. For this was the intent of the wise Rabbi who made them, since poetry is more easily memorized than prose."[74] The anonymous author evokes Sem Tob's message against combatting religious discord with religious oppression by declaring: "the knowledgeable man should not stop teaching his knowledge from fear of suffering difficulties and pain, all the more so because it is known that this [knowledge] comes to the man who has it from divine inspiration."[75] Further on, the author appears to justify the existence

---

71 Shepard, *Shem Tov*, 14.

72 Kaplan, *The Evolution of "Converso" Literature*, 15–19.

73 These reasons are discussed by Kaplan in *The Evolution of "Converso" Literature* and in "The Inception of Limpieza de Sangre (Purity of Blood)".

74 The translation into English is by Perry, *The "Moral Proverbs" of Santob de Carrión*, 174; "Por cuanto syn dubda las dichas trobas son muy notable escritura, que todo omne la deuiera decorar. Ca esta fue la entençion del sabio Raby que las fizo, por que escritura rimada es mejor decorada que non la que va por testo llano" (Perry, 171).

75 The translation into English is by Perry, *The "Moral Proverbs" of Santob de Carrión*, 173; "E por esto non deue çesar de fablar çiençia el que sabe, por cuyta de sofrir trabajos o dolor. Mayormente que es notorio que uyene por devyna ynfluyda de Dios enel omne que la ha" (Perry, 170).

of sectarianism: "Since the Lord God gives wisdom to one so that it can be taught to many, in the same way He could give it [directly] to the many."[76] For all intents and purposes, this attitude lends primacy to the toleration of sectarian rifts in the spirit of preserving social harmony.

Wacks asserts that Sem Tob "invited the audience to consider a world of relativism and pluralism, to hold the contradiction that there may be more than one way to understand this world."[77] Like *Libro de buen amor* by his Christian contemporary, Juan Ruiz, *Proverbios morales* can be understood from different perspectives.[78] Sem Tob's rabbinic voice is thus unique, not only because it is articulated in Castilian rather than Hebrew, but because it incorporates discourse representing both sides of a polemic. It is precisely this multiplicity of interpretations that would have enabled Jewish readers to recognize that Sem Tob meant to be inclusive rather than restrictive and that he urged toleration of internal discord so as to preserve social harmony.

This toleration lies at the core of Sem Tob's response to Abner's inflammatory tone, as he announces early on in *Proverbios morales*:

> I wish to speak, concerning the world and its ways and my doubts about it, very truthful words.
>
> For I am unable to find a mean or reach any decision; I retreat from more than a hundred resolutions every day.
>
> What one man denigrates I see another praise; what this one considers beautiful another finds ugly.
>
> The measuring rod that the buyer calls short, this same rod is called long by the seller.
>
> The one who throws the spear considers it slow, but the man that it reaches finds it speedy enough.[79]

Insofar as multiple interpretations are valid, any Jew might extract a correct one, which is Sem Tob's message of toleration. Sem Tob advocates the necessity of setting aside

---

76 The translation into English is by Perry, *The "Moral Proverbs" of Santob de Carrión*, 173; "pues el señor Dios, commo da la sabiduria a uno para enseñarla a muchos, tan bien la podria dar a los muchos" (Perry, 170).

77 Wacks, *Double Diaspora in Sephardic Literature*, 109. Clark Colahan and Alfred Rodríguez describe the ambiguous tone of *Proverbios morales* in the following terms: "Sem Tob frequently presents opposing points of view and, in keeping with his perception of the relativity of human experience, more than once systematically gives first the arguments for one position and then those for the opposite stance, resolving the conflict only to the extent of endorsing the golden mean" ("Traditional Semitic Forms of Reversibility," 33).

78 On the multiple interpretations of Juan Ruiz's *Libro de buen amor*, see Colahan and Rodríguez, "Traditional Semitic Forms of Reversibility," and Brownlee, *The Status of the Reading Subject*.

79 The translation into English is by Perry, *The "Moral Proverbs" of Santob de Carrión*, 20 (v. 213–29); "Quiero dezir del mundo e de las sus maneras / e cómo de él dubdo palabras muy çerteras, / que non sé tomar tiento nin fazer pleitesía; / de acuerdos más de çiento me torno cada día. / Lo que uno denuesta, veo a otro loallo; / lo que este apuesta, veo a otro afeallo; / la vara que menguada la diz el comprador, / esta mesma, sobrada la diz el vendedor; / el que lança la lança seméjal vagarosa, / pero al que alcança seméjal presurosa" (Carrión, 138 [v. 70a–74b]).

differences only several years before escalating popular anti-Jewish sentiment would result in an outbreak of popular violence in 1355 against the Jews of Toledo, who were targeted because they were perceived as agents of royal oppression. Sem Tob's call for toleration in *Proverbios morales* suggests that he felt that his message not only needed to be delivered to the king but to his fellow Jews as well.

Works Cited

Abner of Burgos (Alfonso de Valladolid). *Mostrador de justicia*. Edited by Walter Mettman. 2 vols. Opladen: Westdeutscher Verlag, 1994–96.
Alfonso, Pedro (Petrus Alphonsi). *Disciplina clericalis*. Edited and translated by Ángel González Palencia. Madrid: Granada, 1948.
Amador de los Ríos, José. *Historia social, política y religiosa de los judíos de España y Portugal*. 3 vols. Madrid: Fortanet, 1874–76.
Baron, Salo Wittmayer. *A Social and Religious History of the Jews*. 18 vols. 2nd ed. New York: Columbia University Press, 1965–83.
Berceo, Gonzalo de. *Milagros de Nuestra Señora*. Edited by Michael Gerli. 5th ed. Madrid: Cátedra, 1991.
——. *Miracles of Our Lady*. Translated by Richard Terry Mount and Annette Grant Cash. Lexington: University Press of Kentucky, 1997.
Brownlee, Marina Scordilis. *The Status of the Reading Subject in the* Libro de buen amor. Chapel Hill: University of North Carolina Press, 1985.
Carrión, Sem Tob de. *Proverbios morales*. Edited by Paloma Díaz-Mas and Carlos Mota. Madrid: Cátedra, 1998.
Cohen, Martin A. "Anan ben David and Karaite Origins." *The Jewish Quarterly Review* 68, no. 3 (January 1978): 129–45.
Colahan, Clark and Alfred Rodríguez. "Traditional Semitic Forms of Reversibility in Sem Tob's *Proverbios morales*." *Journal of Medieval and Renaissance Studies* 13, no. 1 (1983): 33–50.
Daud, Abraham ibn. *The Book of Tradition*. Translated by Gerson D. Cohen. Philadelphia: Jewish Publication Society of America, 1967.
Díaz-Mas, Paloma and Carlos Mota. Introduction to *Proverbios morales*, 11–115. By Sem Tob de Carrión. Edited by Paloma Díaz-Mas and Carlos Mota. Madrid: Cátedra, 1998.
The Disciplina clericalis of Petrus Alfonsi. Translated by P. R. Quarrie. Berkeley: University of California Press, 1977.
García Calvo, Agustín. *Glosas de Sabiduría o Proverbios Morales y otras Rimas*. Madrid: Alianza, 1983.
González, José Maiso, and J. Ramón Lagunilla Alonso. *La judería de Carrión*. Palencia: Cálamo, 2007.
González Llubera, Ignacio. Introduction to *Proverbios morales*, 1–60. By Sem Tob de Carrión. Edited by Ignacio González Llubera. Cambridge: Cambridge University Press, 1947.
Kaplan, Gregory. *El culto a San Millán en Valderredible: Las iglesias rupestres y la formación del Camino de Santiago*. Santander: Goberno de Cantabria, 2007.
——. *The Evolution of "Converso" Literature: The Writings of the Converted Jews of Medieval Spain*. Gainesville: University Press of Florida, 2002.
——. "The Inception of *Limpieza de Sangre* (Purity of Blood) and its Impact in Medieval and Golden Age Spain." In *Marginal Voices: Studies in Converso Literature of Medieval and Golden Age Spain*, 19–41, edited by Amy Aaronson-Friedman and Gregory B. Kaplan. Leiden: Brill, 2012.
Klausner, Joel. "Reflections on Santob de Carrión." *Hispania* 46, no. 2 (May 1963): 304–6.
Kohler, Kaufmann. "Karaites and Karaism." In *The Jewish Encyclopedia*. Edited by Isidore Singer. 12 vols., 7:438–47. New York: KTAV, 1904.
Josephus, Flavius. *The Antiquities of the Jews*. Translated by William Whiston. Accessed November 20, 2018. http://www.gutenberg.org/files/2848/2848-h/2848-h.htm#link 182HCH0001.

———. *The Jewish War*. Translated by G. A. Williamson. Harmondsworth: Penguin, 1970.
León Tello, Pilar. *Los judíos de Palencia*. Madrid: Institución Tello Téllez de Meneses, 1967.
Pérez Celada, Julio A. *Documentación del monasterio de San Zoilo de Carrión (1047–1300)*. Palencia: Garrido Garrido, 1986.
Perry, Theodore Anthony. *The "Moral Proverbs" of Santob de Carrión: Jewish Wisdom in Christian Spain*. Princeton: Princeton University Press, 1987.
Ruiz, Juan. *Libro de buen amor*. Edited by Alberto Blecua. Madrid: Cátedra, 1992.
Sáinz de la Maza, Carlos. "Alfonso de Valladolid y los caraítas: Sobre el aprovechamiento de los textos históricos en la literatura antijudía del siglo XVI." *El Olivo* 31 (1990): 15–32.
Seder Rav 'Amram Gaon bar Sheshna. Jerusalem: Mekhon, 2013.
Shepard, Sanford. *Shem Tov: His World and His Words*. Miami: Universal, 1978.
Stein, Leopold. *Untersuchungen über die Proverbios Morales von Santob de Carrion mit besonderem Hinweis auf die Quellen und Parallelen*. Berlin: Mayer & Müller, 1900.
Szpiech, Ryan. *Conversion and Narrative: Reading and Religious Authority in Medieval Polemic*. Philadelphia: University of Pennsylvania Press, 2012.
Tolan, John. *Petrus Alfonsi and his Medieval Readers*. Gainesville: University Press of Florida, 1993.
Wacks, David A. *Double Diaspora in Sephardic Literature: Jewish Cultural Production Before and After 1492*. Bloomington: Indiana University Press, 2015.

Chapter 4

THE LEGACY OF JEWISH *CUADERNA VÍA* POETRY

SEM TOB'S *PROVERBIOS MORALES* was preserved in five fifteenth-century manuscripts. One of these manuscripts, housed today by the Cambridge University Library as Ms. Add. 3355, contains a fragment in Hebrew *aljamiado* of the so-called "Coplas de Yoçef," which is a fourteenth-century example of an *aljamiado* tradition that began in the thirteenth century with works such as "Cuando el rey Nimrod al campo saldriya."[1] Like this poem, "Coplas de Yoçef" also centres on an Old Testament Patriarch, Joseph, whose life is narrated in forty-two quatrains of what was originally a much longer work.[2] The versification employed in "Coplas de Yoçef" finds parallels with works composed by anonymous thirteenth-century Jewish *cuaderna vía* poets, including the manipulation of the *zéjel* strophic form through the construction of quatrains with *estribillos* that vary greatly, but that always end with the name "Yoçef" (Joseph), as in the following examples:

> And since Joseph knew of his coming,
> he arose quickly and went forth to meet his worthy father.
> He asked for his hand and kissed it.
> Jacob delighted exceedingly in Joseph.

> Then well spake Jacob in this wise:
> "Joy have I seen even were I now to die,
> for I knew not that Joseph was alive.
> Pleased I am today with Joseph, my son."

---

[1] For a discussion of these five manuscripts, see Díaz-Mas and Mota, "Introduction," 11–16. On the features of "Coplas de Yoçef" that indicate that it was composed during the first half of the fourteenth century, see González Llubera, Introduction to *"Coplas de Yoçef"*, xxvi–xxix.

[2] The quatrains are numbered periodically in the manuscript, and the (incomplete) fragment that has been preserved begins with number 261 and ends with number 310.

ABSTRACT In this fourth chapter, "The Legacy of Jewish *Cuaderna Vía* Poetry," I examine texts from the fourteenth century onwards, including original works such as the "Coplas de Yoçef" (Couplets on Joseph) as well as fragments of thirteenth-century texts that have circulated orally outside of the Iberian Peninsula until modern times. When these poems and those analysed in previous chapters are considered together as they are for the first time in this book, they form a unique corpus of Jewish poetry whose origins are grounded in a collaboration between Christians and Jews that has not been recognized in previous scholarship. Readers will find a perspective that challenges the presumption that medieval coexistence was always "predicated upon violence," as David Nirenberg asserts. My analysis reveals that, in Castilian monasteries on the Camino de Santiago where *cuaderna vía* poetry was cultivated, interconfessional toleration was built on a dialogue involving Christian clerical poets writing in tandem with their Jewish counterparts. Judeo-Christian coexistence was predicated on cooperation between Jews and clerics who shared their intellectual formation over a period of time that, as demonstrated by the poems I study, was sufficient enough in length to allow for the process of education to occur repeatedly.

> With great humility thus spake Joseph unto him:
> "To the king thus truly I shall say
> how my father has come unto the city
> and with him Joseph's brethren.
>
> Deske ya lo sopiera Yoçef mui privado
> a reçebir saliera asu padre onrado.
> La mano le pidiera; Luego la ovo besado.
> Mui gran plazer obiera Gakob kon Yoçef.
>
> Gakob luego dezia bien de akesta manera:
> "Vistu e alegria, aun ke agora muera
> ke yo nunka sabia ke Yoçef bivo era;
> Plazer e este dia kon mi figo Yoçef."
>
> Yoçef le dixera kon mui gran omildath:
> "Dire desta manera Al rei por verdath,
> komo venido era Mi padre ala çibdath,
> e ke konel viniera ermanos de Yoçef."[3]

As is evident in González Llubera's transcription into Castilian of the Hebrew *aljamiado*, the composer of "Coplas de Yoçef" utilized consonant rhyme (-ado, -era, -ath) to distinguish the initial three verses in each quatrain as in "Cuando el rey Nimrod al campo saldriya" and "Cuando a Yerušaláyim vide en tanta fatiga." However, in contrast to these poems, "Coplas de Yoçef" consists (with exceptions due to its fragmentary nature) of fourteen-syllable alexandrines, which, like Sem Tob's, differ from those composed by Berceo insofar as they possess internal consonant rhyme between hemistiches in sequential verses (-iera, ia, -era). In the case of "Coplas de Yoçef," the internal consonant rhyme links the first three verses to the *estribillo* to form a quatrain, which speaks again to the conflation of *zéjel* and *cuaderna vía* tendencies in Jewish *cuaderna vía* poetry. Moreover, this internal rhyme, situates "Coplas and Yoçef" and *Proverbios morales* within what González Llubera terms a fourteenth-century "transition between the Alexandrine and a type of hexasyllable that would spring from it" and demonstrates that the authors of both works were aware of contemporary trends.[4]

Like other authors who composed texts in Hebrew *aljamiado*, the author of "Coplas de Yoçef" was adept at manipulating Castilian scansion as revealed in verses from the poem in which there is no contact between word-final and word-initial vowels. Of the one hundred and sixty-eight verses included in the fragment of "Coplas de Yoçef," there are forty-five such verses, including those that form quatrain 267:

> Mi konsego tomedes, mis ermanos mayores:
> Si preguntados fuerdes de reis o de senyores
> Ke sodes, vos diredes, çierto omres pastores:
> E vos non despreçiedes konsego de Yoçef.[5]

---

[3] *"Coplas de Yoçef"*, 7 (v. 264a–66d; the translation into English is by González Llubera).

[4] González Llubera, Introduction to *"Coplas de Yoçef"*, xxix.

[5] "Ye my elder brethren, pay heed unto my counsel: / Should ye be asked by kings or rulers what ye are, / then shall ye answer that surely ye are shepherds. / And Joseph's advice despise ye not" ("Coplas de Yoçef," 9 [v. 267; the translation into English is by González Llubera]).

These verses are all fourteen-syllable alexandrines (as in "Mi-kon-se-go-to-me-des-miser-ma-nos-ma-yo-res"), as are twenty-nine of the forty-five verses in question.

The last verse in the quatrain above, "E vos non despreçiedes konsego de Yoçef" (v. 267d), involves an acute term—the name "Yoçéf"—which, as discussed above with respect to early Jewish *cuaderna vía* poems, requires the addition to the verse of one more syllable according to Castilian norms ("E-vos-non-des-pre-çie-des-kon-se-go-de-Yo-çéf"+1). The composer of "Coplas de Yoçef" uses the same name at the end of other verses that serve as *estribillos*, such as "Apresurada mente respondía Yoçef" ("And straightway Joseph answered"), "Nos todo lo daremos por çivera, Yoçef" ("for food we shall give thee, O Joseph!"), and "En atabud fue puesto, komo mandó Yoçef" ("In a coffin it was laid, as Joseph commanded").[6] It is instructive to point out that, in some final verses of quatrains in which there is no contact between word-final and word-initial vowels, the poet fails to produce fourteen-syllable alexandrines. For example, fifteen syllables are produced in the following verse: "En-ten-dí-an-ke-mer-çe-des-les-fa-zí-a-Yo-çef" (+1).[7] On other occasions, sixteen syllables are produced: "Ke-de-lan-te-ro-ki-sie-ra-ke-pa-sa-sen-de-Yo-çef" (+1).[8] These syllabic variations suggest that the poet had not completely mastered the *cuaderna vía* form, although his goal, to produce fourteen-syllable alexandrines, is clearly evident in verses in which there is no contact between word-final and word-initial vowels. "Coplas de Yoçef" is, like *Proverbios morales*, a fourteenth-century *cuaderna vía* text. Though the influence of the *zéjel* tradition is evident, the lexical variants to the *estribillo* in "Coplas de Yoçef" that consistently result in fourteen-syllable alexandrines testify to the composer's knowledge of Castilian versification, which was likely acquired, as in the cases of other Jewish *cuaderna vía* poets, through interaction with Christian clerics.

The perpetuation of *cuaderna vía* versification occurred in fragmentary texts that were both written down and memorized as exemplified by the contents of a manuscript discovered in 1976 that includes part of *Proverbios morales*.[9] This manuscript is actually a transcription of testimony given before the Inquisition in 1496 by Ferrán Verde, a *converso* who had converted to Catholicism in 1492 in order to avoid being expelled from Spain and who was soon afterwards accused of practising Judaism in secret. During his testimony before the inquisitors, Verde recited two hundred and nineteen stanzas of *Proverbios morales* from memory. This inquisitorial testimony reveals that *Proverbios morales* circulated orally and suggests that a link had developed between the poem and Jewish spirituality. In fact, *Proverbios morales* was employed as a liturgical

---

6 "Coplas de Yoçef," 9 (v. 274a–d), 11 (v. 277d), 19 (v. 287d), respectively (the translations into English are by González Llubera).

7 "[The distraught people] understood that Joseph dealt kindly with them." ("Coplas de Yoçef," 11 [v. 275d; the translation into English is by González Llubera]).

8 "for he wished that Joseph should pass out thense before [them]" ("Coplas de Yoçef," 25 [v. 293d; the translation into English is by González Llubera]).

9 For a discussion of the contents of this manuscript, which is housed today by the Archivo Diocesano de Cuenca as Legajo 6, núm. 125 (CU), see Díaz-Mas and Mota, "Introduction," 15–16.

poem and was sung like a psalm during religious festivals.[10] While originally destined for a royal audience, *Proverbios morales* also continued a tradition exemplified by early Jewish *cuaderna vía* poems such as "Cuando a Yerušaláyim vide en tanta fatiga" of being assimiliated into the Jewish liturgy.

The adoption of Jewish *cuaderna vía* poetry to liturgical uses extended its influence far beyond Jewish communities in northern Spain. One example is a poem in Spanish, "A ti, Señor, rogaré" (To you, Lord, I will Pray), which was first identified in 1797 within a Jewish prayerbook housed by the Valencian monastery of San Miguel de los Reyes. The poem was brought to light by Jesús Antonio Cid, and my English translation of "A ti, Señor, rogaré" is based on his transcription:

1. To you, Lord, I will pray;
   I will ask for mercy from you;
   I will create a prayer for you,
   from me to you each day.

2. I know well
   that you are my creator,
   and that you will be a redeemer
   of my own soul.

3. I committed great sins,
   and I did not attempt to follow
   what the Law says
   for even one day.

4. Ever since I was born
   and came into the world,
   I have always turned
   toward err and obstinacy.

5. My name has been vanity
   ever since I was born;
   will I ever return
   to the place where I used to live?

6. I come to pray to you,
   Lord of mercy;
   may you grant me a place
   where I can return to you.

7. I am infested with earwigs,
   for I have offended the Lord,
   and I must face hardships
   on the cold earth.

8. What will I do now?
   How will I stop myself?
   What kind of reckoning will I make
   with my soul?

---

10 Díaz-Más, "Un género casi perdido," 341–42.

9. They must take me, untouched
to the desolate place.
They must leave me in my burrow
alone, without anyone else.

10. They must place me in dire straits
on the hard earth.
What bitterness this is!
Could anyone withstand this?

11. I sinned, I lied, and I am a fraud
but I always believed in you.
Pardon me,
and I will return to you.

12. [...]
[...]
Time moves in this way,
although I do not know its course.

13. Because if I am not punished
by one of my friends,
my enemy, the one who lead me astray,
will not leave me.

14. [...]
From this day onward without fail,
may pardon be bestowed
upon my soul.

15. Great, noble Lord,
raise your fortress,
pardon us through your nobility,

16. We will return to the grave.
Who will have the strength
to remain without sin
on the Day of Judgement?[11]

---

[11] "1. A ti, Señor, rogaré; / merced te pediré; / oración te faré, / yo a ti cada día. 2. Bien só sabidor / qu'eres mi criador, / tú seas redemidor / d'aquesta alma mía. / 3. Grandes pecados fiz, / e non torcí cerviz / a lo que la Ley diz / atan sólo un día. / 4. Dende que yo nací / e al mundo aparecí, / yo siempre atorcí / en yerro y porfía. / 5. Hebel só yo llamado / dende que fui nado; / ¿qué faré de tornado / tierra como solía? / 6. Vengo t' yo a rogar, / Señor de la piadad, / que m' des algún lugar; / yo a ti tornaría. / 7. Zebratan só yo fecho, / al Señor fis despecho; / meter m' han estrecho / so de la tierra fría. / 8. Hora, ¿yo qué faré, / o qué comidiré, / o qué quenta daré / d'aquesta anima mía? / 9. Levar m' han sin tocado / a lo despoblado; / dejar m' han en mi cado / solo, sin compañía. / 10. Meter m' han n' angostura / so de la tierra dura; / hora, ¡qué amargura / y quién lo sofriría! / 11. Pequé, falso, e mentí / e siempre creí en ti; / perdona tú a mí, / yo a ti tornaría. / 12. [...] / [...] / El tiempo ansí se va / e non sé por qué vía. / 13. Ca sin tomar castigo / de algún mi amigo, / non m' dexa el enemigo / que me atorcía. / 14. [...] De oy sin otro non, / de ti tome perdón / aquesta alma mía. / 15. Señor de gran nobleça, / alça tu fortaleça, / perdónenos tu nobleça, / faz con nós maravilla. / 16. Tornemos a la fuessa, / hora, ¿quién havrá fuerça / para 'star sin vergüença / del Juicio el día" (Cid, "*Lamentación del alma ante la muerte*," 754). Missing verses from the poem are indicated by ellipses.

From the time of its discovery, "A ti, Señor, rogaré," has been considered to be a medieval work composed well before the founding of monastery of San Miguel de los Reyes in 1546.[12] Like early Jewish *cuaderna vía* poems, "A ti, Señor, rogaré" follows the strophic form of the *zéjel*. As such, "A ti, Señor, rogaré" comprises sixteen quatrains in which the initial three verses are distinguished by their consonant rhyme and, in the *zéjel* tradition, are followed by an *estribillo* that maintains a (consonant) rhyme but that varies greatly from stanza to stanza. This variation recalls the deviations from the *zéjel* discussed above in "Cuando el rey Nimrod al campo saldriya" and is one of several features of the poem that situate it within the orbit of Jewish *cuaderna vía* poetry composed during the late thirteenth or early fourteenth centuries among poets accustomed to writing in Hebrew. As in the cases of "Cuando el rey Nimrod al campo saldriya" and "Cuando a Yerušaláyim vide en tanta fatiga," the use of Hebrew terms in "A ti, Señor, rogaré" indicates that the author knew that language. In "A ti, Señor, rogaré," one of these terms, "Hebel" (הֶבֶל [vanity]), is found in verse 5a, and the other term, "Zebratan" (which is a variant of the Hebrew term for "earwig," צַבְתָן [ṣabtān]), appears in verse 7a.[13] In all three poems, a blend of *zéjel* and *cuaderna vía* tendencies is evident.

With respect to the scansion of "A ti, Señor, rogaré," upon taking into consideration verses in which no contact between word-final and word-initial vowels occurs, Cid determines that the predominant verse employed in the poem is "undeniably heptasyllabic," a length that links "A ti, Señor, rogaré" to the same verse length employed by Sem Tob in stanzas 34 to 39 of *Proverbios morales*.[14] The use of heptasyllabic verses in Castilian poetry declined, and all but disappeared, by the end of the 1300s, and the preponderance of these verses in "A ti, Señor, rogaré" suggests, as Cid posits, that it was composed during the first half of that century.[15] The absence of dodecasyllabic verses in "A ti, Señor, rogaré" distances this poem from thirteenth-century works and suggests that, by the fourteenth century, the seven-syllable verse, which is equivalent to one hemistich in a fourteenth-syllable alexandrine, had been mastered by Jewish *cuaderna vía* poets such as the anonymous author of this poem and Sem Tob.

The fact that "A ti, Señor, rogaré" appears in a Jewish prayer book provides additional evidence that Jewish poets were motivated to learn *cuaderna vía* versification in order to compose liturgical poems in Castilian. As a poem appropriate for use in the Jewish liturgy, "A ti, Señor, rogaré" recalls Sem Tob's aforementioned penitential poem for Yom Kippur, in particular with repect to the theme of personal confession, which is expressed in similar

---

[12] In his study of "A ti, Señor, rogare," Cid includes a transcription of the letter that announces the discovery of the poem. In this letter, an estimate of the date of the poem is provided: "It seems that it is not from much later than the thirteenth century" ("No es mui posterior al siglo XIII, según parece" ["*Lamentación del alma ante la muerte*," 731]).

[13] Verse 7a, "I am infested with earwigs," finds a parallel in a poem, "Love Lane," by the nineteenth-century English poet Thomas Hood (b. 1799–d. 1845), in which Hood writes: "'Tis vain to talk of hopes and fears / and hope the least reply to win, / from any maid that stops her ears / in dread of earwigs creeping in!" (*The Complete Poetical Works*, ed. Jerrold, 506).

[14] "indudable base heptasílabica" (Cid, "*Lamentación del alma ante la muerte*," 741).

[15] For a summary of the scholarly opinions regarding the decline of the heptasyllabic verse in fourteenth-century Castilian poetry, see Cid, "*Lamentación del alma ante la muerte*" (744–45).

terms in the two works. For example, Sem Tob's depiction of his lifelong dedication to sin ("I have perverted all the commandments / and my hopes have ended in frustration. / I despaired of finding a remedy for my transgressions / and I ceased seeking repentance") anticipates the depiction of the same lifestyle in "A ti, Señor, rogaré" ("I committed great sins, and I did not attempt to follow / what the Law says / for even one day").[16]

The inclusion of poems such as "A ti, Señor, rogaré" in Jewish prayer books was not the only legacy of Jewish *cuaderna vía* poetry. After the expulsion of Jews from Spain (in 1492) and Portugal (in 1497), communities of Sephardic Jews formed in exile throughout the Mediterranean, where they orally preserved fragments of medieval *cuaderna vía* poems. One such fragment comprises stanzas that derive from the previously discussed poem "El Dio alto que los çielos sostiene," which have been conserved by the Sephardic community of Tetuan. Live revitations of these stanzas were recorded during the 1980s, whereupon they were transcribed by Elena Romero:

> Where are you, Adam? Where are you hiding?
> Did you eat from that tree in full bloom?
> Did you drink water from that river?
> Ah! Blessed God, who dealt with each one differently:
> to the woman he gave painful labour,
> the man would only eat by the sweat of his brow,
> and he made the serpent crawl on its belly.[17]

The first two verses in this passage parallel v. 9b–c in "El Dio alto que los çielos sostiene" ("Where are you, Adam? Where are you hiding? / If you have eaten from the Tree of Wisdom").[18] The final four verses from the fragment above recall v. 12a–d from "El Dio alto que los çielos sostiene," although with a different order in which the three figures appear (woman, man and serpent rather than serpent, woman and man):

> Later on, God convened his court,
> and the serpent was eternally cursed,
> and the woman was given the pain of labour,
> and the man was given a great desire to be dead.[19]

Several verses from "El Dio alto que los çielos sostiene" have also circulated orally for centuries among the Moroccan Jewish community. These verses were recorded during the early 1900s by José Benoliel in his study of Hakitía, the Judeo-Spanish spoken by Moroccan Jews since the arrival of the first refugees from Spain after the expulsion of 1492[20]:

---

16 Shepard, *Shem Tov*, 102.

17 "¿Adóte, Adam, y adónd'estás Escondido? / ¿Si comites de ese árbol tan florido? / ¿Si bebites de ese agua de ese río? / ¡Ay!, bendito Dios, que a cada uno dio su suerte: / y a la mujer que para con dolor fuerte / y al hombre que coma con sudor de su frente / y al culebro que se arrastre sobre su vientre" (Romero, *Coplas sefardíes*, 39).

18 "'¿Dónde estás, Adán? ¿Dónde te as ascondido? / Sy del árbol del saber as comido" (Pescador, "Tres nuevos poemas medievales," 243).

19 "Luego el Dio mandó juntar sus cortes; / al culebro maldíxole las sortes, / e a la muger parir con dolor forte, / e al onbre dio grand lazario [sic] de morte" (Pescador, "Tres nuevos poemas medievales," 244).

20 With regard to the origin of Hakitía, Benoliel writes: "Este dialecto, peculiar a los Judíos de

> Where, Adam, were you hidden?
> Did you eat from that tree in bloom?
> Did you drink from that calm, cool river?
> Did you sin before the holy and blessed Lord?
> "No, Lord, it was the serpent who told me to do it";
> Blessed be He who dealt with each one.
> He made the serpent crawl on its belly;
> He made the woman have a painful labour;
> and He made man work until his death.[21]

The first five verses from this Moroccan fragment recall the content of v. 9b–10d from "El Dio alto que los çielos sostiene":

> "Where are you, Adam? Where are you hiding?
> If you have eaten from the Tree of Wisdom
> By My name, it will cost you dearly.
> He said: "Oh Lord, I was born unlucky!
> The woman you gave me has sold me out;
> she was the one who gave me a fig,
> I have no idea whether it was from the forbidden tree."[22]

The final verses from the Moroccan fragment repeat the order in which the three figures (serpant, woman and man) appear in v. 12a–12d from "El Dio alto que los çielos sostiene." At the same time, there are differences. For example, in the Moroccan fragment, rather than Eve, Adam declares that the serpent has spoken to him, which is evidence of the manner by which oral transmission can modify such a poem. Although oral transmission has changed "El Dio alto que los çielos sostiene," it cannot obscure the legacy of Judeo-Christian coexistence and collaboration on the Camino de Santiago during the thirteenth and fourteenth centuries. In the shadow of Christian clerics who utilized *cuaderna vía* poetry as a vehicle for attracting pilgrims to their monasteries, Jewish poets adapted a Christian medium to their own liturgical and propagandistic ends, as such participating with those clerics in the dissemination of some of the earliest manifestations of Castilian literature.

---

origen ibérico establecidos en Marruecos desde la expulsión de España, y considerablemente distinto del que aún hoy es hablado por los Judíos de Oriente, es un compuesto de castellano antiguo, más o menos bien conservado, de árabe, [y] de hebreo" (*Dialecto judeo-hispano-marroqui o hakitía*, 3).

21 "¿Adó, Adam, estabas escondido? / ¿Comiste de aquel árbol tan florido? / ¿Bebiste de aquel río manso y frío? / ¿Pecaste ante el Señor, santo y bendito? / "No, Señor, que el culebro me lo ha dicho"; / Bendito Él, que dió a cada uno su suerte: / Al culebro arrastrarse sobre el vientre, / A la mujer parir con dolor fuerte, / Al hombre trabajar hasta la muerte" (Benoliel, *Dialecto judeo-hispano-marroqui o hakitía*, 161–62).

22 "'¿Dónde estás, Adán? ¿Dónde te as ascondido? / Sy del árbol del saber as comido, / ¡por el mi nonbre, caro será vendido!' Dixo: '¡Ay, Sennor! ¡Por malo fue [*sic*] nasçido! / La muger que me distes me ay vendido: / de su mano dado me avía vn figo, / no sé sy era del árbol defendido'" (Pescador, "Tres nuevos poemas medievales," 243–44).

Works Cited

Benoliel, José. *Dialecto judeo-hispano-marroqui o hakitía*. Madrid: n.p., 1977.
Berceo, Gonzalo de. *Milagros de Nuestra Señora*. Edited by Michael Gerli. 5th ed. Madrid: Cátedra, 1991.
———. *Miracles of Our Lady*. Translated by Richard Terry Mount and Annette Grant Cash. Lexington: University Press of Kentucky, 1997.
Carrión, Sem Tob de. *Proverbios morales*. Edited by Paloma Díaz-Mas and Carlos Mota. Madrid: Cátedra, 1998.
Cid, Jesús Antonio. "*Lamentación del alma ante la muerte*. Nuevo poema medieval." In *Estudios de folklore y literatura dedicados a Mercedes Díaz Roig*, edited by Beatriz Garza Cuarón and Yvette Jiménez de Báez, 729–91. Ciudad de México: El Colegio de México, 1992.
The Complete Poetical Works of Thomas Hood. Edited by Walter Jerrold. Oxford: Frowde, 1906.
"Coplas de Yoçef": A Medieval Spanish Poem in Hebrew Characters. Edited and translated by Ignacio González Llubera. Cambridge: Cambridge University Press, 1935.
Díaz-Mas, Paloma. "Un género casi perdido de la poesía castellana medieval: La clerecía rabínica." *Boletín de la Real Academia Española* 73 (1993): 329–46.
———, and Carlos Mota. Introduction to *Proverbios morales*, 11–115. By Sem Tob de Carrión. Edited by Paloma Díaz-Mas and Carlos Mota. Madrid: Cátedra, 1998.
González Llubera, Ignacio. Introduction to *"Coplas de Yoçef": A Medieval Spanish Poem in Hebrew Characters*, xi–xxxi. Edited and translated by Ignacio González Llubera. Cambridge: Cambridge University Press, 1935.
Manuscript Add. 3355. 15th century. Cambridge University Library, Cambridge.
Manuscript Legajo 6, núm. 125 (CU). Archivo Diocesano de Cuenca, Cuenca.
Pescador, María del Carmen. "Tres nuevos poemas medievales." *Nueva Revista de Filología Hispánica* 14 (1960): 242–50.
Romero, Elena, ed. *Coplas sefardíes: Primera selección*. Córdoba: El Almendro, 1988.
Shepard, Sanford. *Shem Tov: His World and His Words*. Miami: Universal, 1978.

CONCLUSION

THE PREVIOUS CHAPTERS in this book describe the process by which Jewish writers adopted a Christian poetic mode that was popularized by clerics. One issue that merits consideration is the reception by these Jewish writers of anti-Semitic Christian *cuaderna vía* discourse. For example, it is interesting to ponder how Jews of the thirteenth and fourteenth centuries might have reacted to hearing anti-Semitic episodes from *Milagros*, which may have occurred if Berceo's work was used as a model for instruction. Whether or not there was some reluctance among Jews to imitate a type of poetry that exploited anti-Semitic libels, this did not dissuade them as the works considered in this book testify. Moreover, any trepidation felt by these Jews did not discourage them from entering monasteries and studying with Christian clerics. Jews undoubtedly placed a value on learning *cuaderna vía* poetry for its capacity to disseminate information through a metrical form whose rhyme facilitated memorization.

The incorporation of *cuaderna vía* poems into the Jewish liturgy indicates that they enjoyed a widespread appeal, and it would be logical to conclude that these poems were used as such because of their performative character. The Jewish liturgy involves numerous hymns and prayers that are sung aloud by congregants and their spiritual leaders (rabbis or cantors), and the tendency for Christian clerical *cuaderna vía* poetry to be publicly performed may have encouraged Jews to imitate both its metrical structure and mode of dissemination.[1] Additionally, the requirement for Jews to engage in communal worship may also have played a pivotal role in the popularization of Jewish *cuaderna vía* liturgical poems. According to the Talmud, Jews are obligated to pray aloud in a quorum of ten adults on certain occasions, including when reading from the Torah and when reciting prayers such as the Amidah.[2] In light of this obligation, it is easy to envision how *cuaderna vía* poems, which Christian clerics also read aloud in group settings, were assimilated into the Jewish liturgy.

The fact that Jewish *cuaderna vía* poetry evolved over the course of the thirteenth and fourteenth centuries speaks to the impact of coexistence on the formation of a sub-genre of medieval Castilian literature that passed through two stages of development. Poems that pertain to the first stage, including "El Dio alto que los çielos sostiene," "Cuando el rey Nimrod al campo saldriya," and "Cuando a Yerušaláyim vide en tanta fatiga," appear to date from the thirteenth century. These poems incorporate markers of Castilian *cuaderna vía* poetry, in particular the quatrains, consonant rhyme and vense length that evolved from study with Cluniac monks who taught at Castilian monasteries (or with Spanish clerics taught by Cluniac monks). Christian and Jewish poems of the thirteenth century reveal a difference between their respective verse lengths, and

---

[1] On the link between *cuaderna vía* poetry and public performance, see Kinkade, who describes such performances as "mimes recitation[s]" ("Sermon in the Round," 134), Perry, *Art and Meaning*, 141, and Goldberg, "The Voice of the Author," 107.

[2] On the Talmudic requirement for a quorum of ten Jewish worshipers, see Allen, *Further Perspectives on Jewish Law*, 52–55.

this difference may be due to distinct manners of perceiving the French texts that were used as models. The fourteen-syllable alexandrine verse thus became a standard among Christian poets before it did among Jews, who at first imitated directly their French models by composing dodecasyllabic verses, and who did not become adept at the fourteen-syllable alexandrine until the fourteenth century. Jews took more time to develop Castilian writing skills because they were accustomed to writing in Hebrew.

As a result, a tendency that defines the first stage in Jewish *cuaderna vía* poetry is the use of Hebrew terms. Their appearance in poems written in Hebrew *aljamiado*, including "Cuando el rey Nimrod al campo saldriya" and "Cuando a Yerušaláyim vide en tanta fatiga," indicates that Jewish poets writing during the first stage were novices at composing works in Castilian. These writers were working during the thirteenth century, contemporary to the Christian clerics who composed the earliest *cuaderna vía* poems. Gonzalo de Berceo is, in fact, the first Castilian poet to reveal his name, and he and Jewish contemporaries, who were influenced by French Cluniac monastic culture, participated in forging a new literary genre in a language for which there were very few texts on which they could model their discourse.[3] These writers learned to reproduce in writing the acoustic norms for dividing syllables in Castilian, and "A ti, Señor, rogaré," a Spanish poem that also incorporates Hebrew terms, may be considered a transitional work between the thirteenth and fourteenth centuries in light of its tendency toward heptasyllabic verses, which reveals a progression toward the fourteen-syllable alexandrine.

Hebrew terms do not appear in "Coplas de Yoçef" or *Proverbios morales*, which were composed during the second stage of Jewish *cuaderna vía* poetry. In this context, it is instructive to point out that, while "Coplas de Yoçef" is written in Hebrew characters, no Hebrew term is found in the fragment of the poem that has been preserved. The lack of Hebrew terms in "Coplas de Yoçef" and *Proverbios morales*, and the use in these works of fourteen-syllable rather than twelve-syllable alexandrines, reveals that Jewish *cuaderna vía* poetry evolved over the course of the thirteenth and fourteenth centuries. The transition to the fourteen-syllable alexandrine indicates that Jews became more skilled at composing poetry in Castilian. This may have been a result of the fact that Jews were taught during the fourteenth century by Castilian clerics rather than French Cluniac monks, whose presence in monastic schools would have grown less frequent as the influence of Cluny waned.

An evolution is not only evident in the length of the alexandrines used in Jewish *cuaderna vía* poems, but also in the length of the poems themselves. The number of stanzas in the three poems from the first stage, as well as in "A ti, Señor, rogaré," ranges between fourteen and eighteen. Poems from the second stage are much longer. The forty-two quatrains preserved from "Coplas de Yoçef" represent a fraction of a work that originally contained more than three hundred, and *Proverbios morales*, though not comprising quatrains, contains more than 1400 fourteen-syllable alexandrines. The length and versification of these poems suggests that, over time, instruction by Christian clerics in *cuaderna vía* poetry became more sophisticated. This instruction was undoubt-

---

3 "Yo maestro Gonçalvo de Verceo nomnado" (Berceo, *Milagros*, 69 [v. 2a]; "I, Master Gonzalo de Berceo" [Berceo, *Miracles*, 21 (v. 2a); the translation into English is by Mount and Cash]).

edly successful as exemplified by Sem Tob's mastery of hiatus in *Proverbios morales*. It is also clearly evident that Jews received instruction from Christian clerics on a regular basis, which speaks to lasting coexistence.

The textual and historical evidence that situates this coexistence within Castilian monastic schools on the Camino de Santiago defines these schools as places for interaction and, by extension, toleration between two cultures during the thirteenth and fourteenth centuries. A significant contribution to the success of this coexistence was made by the collaboration between Spanish and French clerics that provided a new form of edification and entertainment to pilgrims, thus increasing their numbers and the economic prosperity that pilgrimage offered. This prosperity, in turn, contributed to the growth of Jewish communities around key pilgrimage monasteries, which afforded Jews opportunities to interact with Christian clerics. This interaction was fruitful and was a frequent occurrence as the evolution of Jewish *cuaderna vía* poetry demonstrates. As the period during which Jews studied *cuaderna vía* poetry with Christian clerics in Castilian monastic schools came to an end, Sem Tob's *Proverbios morales* rivals the artistry of Berceo's *Milagros*, which serves as enduring testimony of the value of interconfessional collaboration. Although the Jewish communities around Castilian monasteries were destroyed by the end of the fifteenth century, the legacy of an extended period of coexistence resonates in the dissemination of Jewish *cuaderna vía* poems until modern times.

Works Cited

Allen, Wayne. *Further Perspectives on Jewish Law and Contemporary Issues*. Bloomington: Trafford, 2011.

Berceo, Gonzalo de. *Milagros de Nuestra Señora*. Edited by Michael Gerli. 5th ed. Madrid: Cátedra, 1991.

———. *Miracles of Our Lady*. Translated by Richard Terry Mount and Annette Grant Cash. Lexington: University Press of Kentucky, 1997.

Carrión, Sem Tob de. *Proverbios morales*. Edited by Paloma Díaz-Mas and Carlos Mota. Madrid: Cátedra, 1998.

"Coplas de Yoçef": A Medieval Spanish Poem in Hebrew Characters. Edited and translated by Ignacio González Llubera. Cambridge: Cambridge University Press, 1935.

Goldberg, Harriet. "The Voice of the Author in the Works of Gonzalo de Berceo and in the *Libro de Alexandre* and the *Poema de Fernán González*." *La corónica* 8, no. 2 (1980): 100–12.

Kinkade, Richard P. "Sermon in the Round: the Mester de Clercía as Dramatic Art." In *Studies in Honor of Gustavo Correa*, edited by Charles B. Faulhaber, Richard P. Kinkade and Theodore A. Perry, 127–36. Potomac: Scripta Humanistica, 1986.

Perry, Theodore Anthony. *Art and Meaning in Berceo's "Vida de Santa Oria"*. New Haven: Yale University Press, 1968.

INDEX

Abraham ibn Daud *see* Daud
Abu'l-Taras, Cid: 56, 57
"A ti, Señor, rogaré": 70–73, 78
Abner (Alfonso de Valladolid), Jewish theologian (b. ca. 1270–d. ca. 1347): 57–62
  Mostrador de justicia: 57–58, 64
Aguilar de Campóo, town near Palencia: 13
Alexander the Great, ancient king of Macedon: 1, 9, 15
Alexandre de Bernay *see* Bernay
Alfácar, Josef, royal physician: 60
Alfonso VI, king of León
  (b. ca. 1040–d. 1109): 12, 21, 54, 57
Alfonso VII, king of Castile and León
  (r. 1126–1157): 60
Alfonso VIII, king of Castile
  (r. 1158–1214): 60
Alfonso XI, king of Castile (r. 1312–1350): 4, 43, 47, 60–61
Alphonsi, Petrus (Pedro Alfonso), convert from Judaism to Christianity: 49–50, 64
  Disciplina clericalis: 49–51, 64
Anan ben David *see* David
Apollonius of Tyre *see* Tyre

Beato de Liébana *see* Liébana
Berceo, Gonzalo de, cleric of San Millán de la Cogolla (b. ca. 1196–d. ca. 1260): 2–3, 5, 15, 23–25, 68, 77–78, 80
  Milagros de Nuestra Señora: 5, 18, 22, 24, 51–53, 64, 75, 78–80
Bernard of Cluny *see* Cluny
Bernay, Alexandre de, French poet: 9, 16, 24
Becket, Thomas, martyr (b. 1118–d. 1170): 9
Breviarium apostolorum: 10
Brunetto Latini *see* Latini

Camino de Santiago, pilgrimage route:
  1–4, 10–11, 13, 15, 18, 21–23, 25, 27, 43–45, 64, 67, 70, 74, 79

Carrión, Sem Tob de, poet
  (b. ca. 1290–d. ca. 1369):
  3, 5, 43, 46–50, 60,
  "Debate between the Pen and the Scissors": 46
  Proverbios morales: 47–53, 59–62, 64, 75, 80
Carrión de los Condes, town near Palencia:
  3–4, 11–12, 23, 43–46, 51, 54, 57–58, 60, 64
  San Zoilo (monastery): 13, 25, 27, 43–46, 64
Castrojeriz, town near Burgos: 23
Cervatos, town in Cantabria: 13, 44
La Chanson de Roland: 21, 24
Charlemagne, Holy Roman emperor: 7
Chrétien de Troyes *see* Troyes
Cid *see* Abu'l-Taras
Cluny, monastery in Burgundy and order:
  1–2, 5, 7–9, 11–13, 22, 24–25, 27, 44, 46, 78
Cluny, Bernard of, monk and author: 24,
Codex Calixtinus see Liber Sancti Jacobi
Conrad de Hirsau *see* Hirsau
Conversos: 61, 64, 69
"Coplas de Yoçef": 4–5, 67–69, 75, 78, 80
Cuaderna vía, verse form: 1–4, 7, 15–23, 27–28, 31–32, 37–41, 43–47, 51–54, 67–74, 77–79
"Cuando el rey Nimrod al campo saldriya": 32–39, 51, 67–68, 72, 77–78
"Cuando a Yerušaláyim vide en tanta fatiga": 38–40, 51, 68, 70, 72, 77–78

Daud, Abraham ibn, Cordovan historian and philosopher
  (b. ca. 1110–d. ca. 1180): 56–58, 64
David, Anan ben, Karaite leader
  (b. ca. 715–d. ca. 795): 55–56, 64
"Debate between the Pen and the Scissors" *see* Carrión, Sem Tob de

De contemptu mundi, literary genre: 9, 24
Dialogus super auctores see Hirsau
Diego Gelmírez *see* Gelmírez
"El Dio alto que los çielos sostiene": 28–34, 36–37, 51, 73–74
Disciplina clericalis see Alphonsi

Enrique II, king of Castile (r. 1369–1379): 47
Ezra, Yehuda ben, rabbi and royal steward (r. 1126–1157): 60

La fazienda de ultra mar: 30, 42
Fernán González *see* González
Fernando III, king of Castile (r. 1217–1252): 27, 45
Ferrán Verde *see* Verde
Ferruziel, Joseph ha Nasi ibn, rabbi and royal physician (d. ca. 1145): 57, 60
Flavius Josephus *see* Josephus
Frómista, town near Palencia: 23, 27, 46
  San Martín (church): 12–13, 23, 27

García, Pedro, priest in Carrión de los Condes: 46
Gelmírez, Diego, archbishop of Compostela (b. ca. 1069–d. ca. 1140): 11
González, Fernán, first count of Castile (d. 970): 15
Gonzalo de Berceo *see* Berceo
Guernes de Pont-Sainte-Maxence *see* Pont-Sainte-Maxence
Guglielmo da Volpiano *see* Volpiano

Ibn Hazm *see* Hazm

Hakitía, Judeo-Spanish language: 73–75
Hazm, Ibn, Muslim historian and theologian (b. 994–d. 1064): 56
Hilay, Natronay bar, Jewish scholar in Sura (b. ca. 795–d.ca. 865): 56
Hirsau, Conrad de, Cluniac author (b. ca. 1070–d. ca. 1150)
  Dialogus super auctores: 18, 25
Hugh the Great, abbot of Cluny (b. 1024–d. 1109): 12, 21

James ("the Great", son of Zebedee), saint: 10–11
Josef ibn Sasón *see* Sasón
Joseph ha Nasi ibn Ferruziel *see* Ferruziel
Josephus, Flavius, Romano-Jewish historian (b. 37–d. ca. 100): 55, 64

Karaism: 56–60, 64

Lambert li Tors *see* Tors
Latini, Brunetto, Italian philosopher (b. ca. 1220–d. ca. 1294): 10, 25
Libro de Alexandre: 15–18, 22, 24–25
Libro de buen amor see Ruiz
Libro de miseria de omne: 18–20, 22, 24–25
Liber Sancti Jacobi / Codex Calixtinus: 11, 25
Liébana, Beato de, Cantabrian monk (b. ca. 730–d. ca. 800): 10, 24

Maqāmā, Arabic literary form: 46
Mauregato, Asturian monarch (r. 783–788): 10
Milagros de Nuestra Señora see Berceo
Mostrador de justicia see Abner
Morval, Bernard of *see* Cluny, Bernard of

Nahawandi, Benjamin, Karaite scholar: 56
Natronay bar Hilay *see* Hilay

Pablo de Santa María
  see Santa María, Pablo de
Palencia
  Jewish community: 43, 45–46, 54, 57
  university: 15–16
Pedro I ("the Cruel"), king of Castile and León (r. 1350–1369): 4, 43, 47–49, 53, 59, 61, 64
Pedro García *see* García
Peter the Venerable, abbot of Cluny (b. ca. 1092–d. 1156): 8
Petrus Alphonsi *see* Alphonsi
Pharisees, Jewish religious school: 54–55
Pijo, Baru, Jewish resident of Carrión de los Condes: 46
Pont-Sainte-Maxence, Guernes de, French poet (fl. twelfth century): 9, 16, 25
Proverbios morales see Carrión, Sem Tob de

Rabbinism, Jewish religious school: 54–55, 58–60
Ruiz, Juan
　Libro de buen amor: 22–23, 26, 62, 64–65
Ruta Románica, pilgrimage route: 13, 19

Sadducees, Jewish religious school: 55, 58
Sahagún, town near León: 13
Samuel ben Josef ibn Sasón *see* Sasón
San Martín (church) *see* Frómista
San Martín de Elines (monastery/collegiate church) *see* Valderredible
San Miguel de los Reyes (monastery) *see* Valencia
San Millán de la Cogolla (monastery in La Rioja): 2, 13, 15, 18, 25, 44, 64
San Zoilo (monastery) *see* Carrión de los Condes
Santa María, Pablo de (Solomon ha Levi), rabbi and convert (b. ca. 1351–d. 1435): 61
Santa María de las Huelgas (monastery near Burgos): 27
Santiago of Compostela, city in Galicia *see* Camino
Sasón, Josef ibn, Jewish poet (d. 1336): 46–47
Sem Tob de Carrión *see* Carrión, Sem Tob de
Solomon ha Levi *see* Santa María, Pablo de

Talmud: 46, 55–59, 77
Thomas Becket *see* Becket
Tors, Lambert li, French poet (fl. twelfth century): 9, 26, 41–42
Tournai, city in Hainaut: 7
　St. Martin (monastery): 7, 27
Troyes, Chrétien de, French poet (fl. ca. 1160–1191): 21
Tyre, Apollonius of, legendary classical character: 15

Valderredible, municipality in Cantabria: 13, 25, 64
　San Martín de Elines (monastery/collegiate church): 13, 19–20, 25
Valencia, city in Spain
　San Miguel de los Reyes / Sant Miquel dels Reis (monastery): 70, 72
Verbiginale: 16, 26
Verde, Ferrán, convert to Christianity in 1492: 69
La Vie de Saint Alexis: 21, 26
Volpiano, William of, Cluniac reformer (b. 962–d. 1031): 9

William I, duke of Aquitaine (b. 875–d. 918): 7

Zéjel, Islamic literary genre: 37, 40, 67–69, 72